Made with ♥ on the Notion Press Platform

www.notionpress.com

A Text Book On SOFTWARE PROJECT MANAGEMENT

Authors
Mr. N.Udayakumar
Dr.A.Saritha
Dr.S.Thirumal
Dr.A.Manikandan

Editor
Dr.N.Kumar

DEDICATION

To Our Beloved Families, Dear Friends, and Inspiring Students,

With deepest appreciation for your unwavering support, encouragement, and understanding throughout this journey.

By Authors

Mr.N.Udayakumar

Dr.A.Saritha

Dr.S.Thirumal

Dr.A.Manikandan

About the Authors

Mr. N. Udayakumar is an Assistant Professor in the Department of Computer Science and Engineering at Vels Institute of Science Technology and Advanced Studies (VISTAS). He has a Bachelor of Engineering in Computer Science and Engineering and a Master of Engineering in Computer and Communication. He is now wrapping up his Ph.D. study in malware analysis, with a focus on computer networks, network security, cyber security, and cyber forensics.

Dr.A.Saritha works as an Assistant Professor in the Department of Computer Science and Engineering at Vels Institute of Science Technology and Advanced Studies (VISTAS). She holds a Bachelor of Engineering in Computer Science and Engineering, a Master of Engineering in Computer Science and Engineering and Ph.D in MANET. Her area of specialization is MANET, Computer Networks, Software Engineering, Big Data Analytics.

Dr. S. Thirumal is currently working as an Assistant Professor in the department of Computer Science and Engineering, Vels Institute of Science, Technology and Advanced Studies, Chennai, has about 13 years of teaching experience. He obtained his Ph.D degree in computer science and engineering in the year 2023 from Hindustan Institute of Technology and Science (HITS), Chennai. He has published 26 research papers in refereed international journals and various international conferences. His research areas are Big Data Analytics, Computer Network, Cloud Computing, Image Processing, Network Security & Machine Learning.

Dr.A.Manikandan is an Assistant Professor in the Department of Computer Science and Engineering at Vels Institute of Science Technology and Advanced Studies (VISTAS). He has a Bachelor of Technology in Information Technology, a Master of Engineering in CSE, and a Ph.D. in Big Data Analytics. His areas of specialization include computer networks, network security, cyber security, and IoT. He has published 36 research publications.

Editor Spotlight

Dr. N. Kumar currently working as a Professor in Vels Institute of Science, Technology and Advanced Studies, Chennai. He obtained his Ph.D degree in computer science and engineering in 2015 at Karpagam University, Coimbatore. He has totally 17 years of teaching experience in the field of Computer Science and Engineering. He has published 83 articles in international journals and presented 46 papers in the international conferences. His research areas are Computer Network, Mobile Adhoc Networks, WSN, Cloud Computing, Image Processing , Network Security, Big Data Analytics & Machine Learning.

Contents

Foreword

In today's fast-paced digital landscape, the successful delivery of software projects is not just a measure of organizational efficiency but a testament to the agility and adaptability of teams. This textbook on software project management comes at a critical juncture when the demand for robust methodologies and skilled practitioners is higher than ever before.

Evolution and Complexity

Software development has evolved from a niche field to a cornerstone of modern business operations. As organizations strive to innovate and stay competitive, the ability to manage software projects effectively has become paramount. This book provides a comprehensive roadmap for navigating the complexities of software project management, offering insights that are both timeless and forward-thinking.

Guidance for Practitioners

Whether you are a seasoned project manager or a budding software engineer, this textbook equips you with the tools, techniques, and frameworks necessary to tackle challenges head-on. From initiating projects with clarity to executing them with precision and delivering value consistently, each chapter distills years of industry experience into practical guidance.

Adaptability in a Changing World

The field of software project management is not static. It evolves alongside technological advancements, shifting market demands, and emerging methodologies. This textbook not only covers established practices but also explores agile methodologies, DevOps principles, and other cutting-edge approaches that empower teams to respond swiftly to change and deliver results effectively.

Interactive Learning

Embedded within these pages are real-world case studies, thought-provoking exercises, and actionable insights designed to bridge the gap between theory and practice. Whether you are studying in a classroom or enhancing your skills independently, the interactive nature of this textbook encourages active engagement and deepens your understanding of key concepts.

Collaborative Effort

The creation of this textbook has been a collaborative effort, bringing together the expertise and passion of educators, industry professionals, and researchers. Their collective insights have shaped a resource that not only educates but also inspires a new generation of software project managers to excel in their roles.

Looking Ahead

As you embark on your journey through this textbook, embrace the challenges and opportunities that lie ahead. Software project management is not just about managing tasks; it's about empowering teams, fostering innovation, and driving meaningful outcomes. May this book serve as your compass, guiding you towards success in your software project management endeavors.

Feedback and Community

Your feedback is invaluable to us. As you engage with the content, we encourage you to share your thoughts, questions, and experiences. Together, we can continue to refine and improve this textbook, ensuring its relevance and impact in an ever-changing industry landscape.

Conclusion

we extend our gratitude for choosing this textbook as your companion on the journey of mastering software project management. May it empower you to lead with confidence, innovate with purpose, and deliver excellence in every project you undertake.

Preface

Welcome to the world of Software Project Management! In an era where technology evolves at an unprecedented pace, the ability to manage software projects efficiently and effectively has become crucial for organizations worldwide. This textbook is designed to be your comprehensive guide through the intricacies of planning, executing, and delivering successful software projects.

Intended Audience

This book is intended for students studying software engineering, computer science, or related disciplines, as well as professionals entering or currently working in the field of software project management. Whether you are a novice seeking foundational knowledge or an experienced practitioner looking to refine your skills, this text offers insights that cater to diverse levels of expertise.

Structure and Approach

The book begins by laying a solid foundation with fundamental concepts and principles of software project management. It then progresses to cover advanced topics such as risk management, agile methodologies, stakeholder communication, and quality assurance. Each chapter is structured to provide both theoretical insights and practical strategies, ensuring that you not only understand key concepts but also learn how to apply them in real-world scenarios.

Key Features

- **Case Studies:** Illustrative examples and case studies drawn from industry experiences provide practical insights into challenges and solutions encountered in software project management.
- **Tools and Techniques:** Discussions on popular tools and techniques used in the industry, equipping you with the knowledge to leverage them effectively.
- **Emerging Trends:** Exploration of emerging trends and technologies shaping the future of software project management, keeping you informed about the latest developments in the field.

Acknowledgments

The book "Software Project Management" was a collaborative effort that benefitted from the expertise of the authors and the meticulous evaluation and constructive feedback provided by **Dr. N. Kumar**, a Professor at the Department of Computer Science and Technology at Vels Institute of Science Technology and Advanced Studies (VISTAS). Our families, colleagues, and the publishing team also played vital roles, offering unwavering encouragement and support. We are grateful for the professionalism and dedication of the publishing team in bringing this book to fruition.

Chapter 1

INTRODUCTION TO SOFTWARE PROJECT MANAGEMENT

Introduction

Software project management encompasses the comprehension of efficient planning, organization, and resource management in order to achieve successful completion of software projects. It includes a range of strategies, techniques, and tools designed to accomplish project objectives while considering limitations such as time, budget, and scope.

Important components of software project management encompass:

1. Project Planning is the process of defining the project's scope, objectives, and deliverables. This entails delineating tasks, assessing resources, and formulating schedules.
2. Resource management involves the allocation and supervision of human resources, equipment, and materials that are required for the project.
3. Risk management involves the identification of potential hazards, evaluation of their consequences, and formulation of solutions to minimize their impact.
4. Communication: Ensuring unambiguous and efficient communication among team members, stakeholders, and clients during the whole duration of the project.
5. Quality Management involves the implementation of mechanisms to ensure that the software adheres to quality standards and fulfills user expectations.
6. Change Management: Managing alterations to project scope, timeline, or resources with the goal of minimizing disturbance.
7. Monitoring and control involves closely observing the progress made in relation to the established plan, detecting any deviations from the expected course, and implementing any remedial measures.
8. Documentation: Ensuring the meticulous maintenance of extensive records pertaining to project plans, requirements, designs, and test cases.
9. Software Development Methodologies: Employing methodologies such as Agile, Waterfall, or Hybrid approaches to organize and carry out the development process.
10. Project Closure involves the formalization of project completion, the performing of post-project reviews, and the capture of lessons learned for future improvement.

Efficient software project management requires the harmonious integration of technical proficiency, leadership abilities, and effective communication skills in order to successfully produce superior software within the designated timeframe and financial constraints. Successful achievement of project objectives necessitates collaboration among team members and stakeholders to effectively overcome hurdles.

1.1 Project Definition

A project definition, alternatively referred to as a project charter or project brief, is a fundamental document that delineates the goal, objectives, scope, stakeholders, and beginning planning for a project. It functions as a strategic plan and formal agreement between the individuals involved in the project and the team responsible for its execution. The project definition normally comprises the following essential components:

1. Project Purpose: A concise statement that explains the rationale behind initiating the project and the anticipated advantages or results.
2. Objectives refer to the specific and quantifiable targets that the project strives to accomplish. Objectives should adhere to the SMART criteria, which means they should be specific, achievable, relevant, and time-bound.
3. Scope refers to the specific boundaries and limitations of a project, determining what is encompassed within it and what is excluded. It establishes limits and provides clear definitions of the expected outcomes, assignments, available resources, and limitations.
4. Stakeholders are individuals, groups, or organizations who are involved in or impacted by the project. This encompasses both internal stakeholders (team members, management) and external stakeholders (customers, users, suppliers).
5. Constraints and Assumptions refer to several factors that can impose limitations on the execution of a project or influence its final result. These factors can include budgetary constraints, time limitations, resource availability, or technical limitations. Assumptions are unverified circumstances that are thought to be true.
6. Milestones and Deliverables refer to significant milestones or accomplishments that indicate the advancement in finishing the project. Deliverables refer to concrete outputs or outcomes that the project will generate.
7. Risks and Dependencies refer to potential events or difficulties that have the potential to affect the success of the project. They also include external elements or tasks that need to be performed before specific project activities may move forward.
8. Project Team: This document outlines the specific roles and responsibilities of the team members involved in the project, which include the project manager, stakeholders, and any other essential people.
9. Approach and Methodology: This section provides an outline of the strategies, procedures, or processes that will be employed to effectively oversee and carry out the project.
10. Approval refers to the endorsement or confirmation from the appropriate stakeholders or sponsors, expressing their agreement with the project definition and their commitment to support its execution.

Developing a thorough project definition is crucial to guaranteeing clarity, alignment of expectations, and the successful execution of the project. It acts as a point of reference during the whole project duration to ensure that the team remains focused on accomplishing the mutually agreed objectives and deliverables.

1.2 Contract Management

Contract management in software project management entails the supervision and management of contracts between different parties participating in a software project. The parties involved in these events may consist of the customer, vendors, subcontractors, and other stakeholders. Efficient contract management guarantees that all parties strictly follow the terms and conditions specified in the contracts, thereby reducing risks, assuring adherence to regulations, and facilitating successful project completion.

Key Points of Contract Management:

1. Contract Creation: This entails composing contracts that precisely delineate the extent of work, project deliverables, timetables, payment arrangements, and any other pertinent terms and conditions. It is crucial to guarantee that contracts are thorough, legally valid, and in line with the project goals.
2. Contract Negotiation: Prior to concluding contracts, talks may occur to resolve any differences, elucidate terms, or bargain over terms and pricing. Proficiency in communication and negotiation is essential at this phase in order to achieve mutually agreeable resolutions.
3. Contract Review: After negotiations, contracts are subjected to a comprehensive examination by legal professionals or contract managers to guarantee precision, uniformity, and adherence to legal and regulatory obligations.
4. Contract Execution: Following careful examination and endorsement, contracts are signed by all relevant parties, therefore legally obligating them to the mutually agreed-upon terms and conditions.
5. Contract Monitoring: Contract managers oversee the performance of all parties involved in the project to verify that they are meeting their contractual responsibilities. This includes monitoring and documenting the progress of deliverables, milestones, timetables, and budgets as specified in the contract.
6. Change Management: As projects advance, there could arise modifications in the scope, requirements, or other elements that require adjustments to contracts. Contract managers supervise the change management process, guaranteeing that any alterations are recorded, authorized, and included into the current contracts.
7. Risk management involves the identification and mitigation of potential risks related to contracts, including issues such as non-compliance, conflicts, or delays. They can employ risk mitigation tactics and contingency plans to successfully tackle these hazards.
8. Contract Closure: Upon project completion, contract managers verify the fulfillment of all contractual duties and the acceptance of final deliverables by the client. Contracts are

then terminated in a formal manner, and any remaining payments or unresolved matters are handled.

9. Documentation and record-keeping are crucial for the whole duration of a contract to meticulously monitor all conversations, modifications, and transactions associated with the contracts. This facilitates the resolution of conflicts and promotes transparency and accountability.

Efficient contract management is essential for the successful implementation of software projects, as it aids in risk reduction, guarantees adherence to regulations, and promotes harmonious relationships among all stakeholders.

1.3 Activities Covered by Software Project Management

Software project management involves a diverse set of tasks focused on the planning, organization, management, and control of software projects to guarantee the successful delivery of software products or solutions. The following are the primary activities commonly encompassed by software project management:

1. **Commencement of the project:**

- Project Definition involves clearly establishing the scope, objectives, deliverables, and stakeholders of a project.
- Feasibility Study: Evaluating the project's technical, economic, and operational viability.
- A project charter is a formal document that grants authority to a project and outlines its starting criteria.

2. **Project Planning:**

- Scope Management involves the process of precisely defining the boundaries of a project by determining what is included and what is omitted from the project scope.
- A Work Breakdown Structure (WBS) is a method of dividing the project deliverables into smaller, more manageable tasks.
- Scheduling involves the creation of a project schedule that clearly defines the tasks, dependencies, milestones, and deadlines.
- Resource Planning involves the identification and allocation of the necessary resources (such as human, financial, and equipment) required for a project.
- Risk management involves the identification of prospective risks, the evaluation of their potential impact and likelihood, and the development of strategies to address them.
- Quality Planning involves the establishment of quality objectives and processes to ensure that the software satisfies the given requirements.

- Communication Planning is the process of determining the specific communication channels, frequency, and stakeholders that will be involved in the project's communication activities.

3. Implementation of the project:

- Task Execution involves the implementation of tasks in accordance with the project strategy and timeline.
- Team Management: Overseeing the dynamics, roles, duties, and performance of a team.
- Progress monitoring involves closely monitoring the advancement of a project, finding any deviations from the planned course, and implementing appropriate remedial measures.
- Quality Assurance involves the systematic monitoring and verification of project outcomes to ensure that they fulfill the established quality standards.
- Change management involves the effective management of modifications to project scope, timeline, or resources in order to minimize any negative effects on project goals.
- Project Monitoring and Control refers to the process of overseeing and managing a project to ensure that it is progressing according to plan and within the defined parameters.
- Performance Monitoring is the ongoing measurement of project performance in relation to established baselines and objectives.
- Status Reporting: Consistently informing stakeholders about the ongoing progress, challenges, and potential hazards of the project.
- Issue and Risk Management: The process of identifying and resolving problems and mitigating potential risks at every stage of the project's lifespan.
- Change Control involves the examination and authorization of modifications to the project's scope, timeline, or resources.
- Quality Control involves the process of testing and verifying the software to ensure that it fulfills the specific quality standards.

4. Conclusion of the Project:

- Handover and Delivery: The process of transferring completed work to stakeholders and ensuring that they accept it.
- Key Takeaways: Recording accomplishments, difficulties, and insights gained from a project for the benefit of future endeavors.
- Concluding Activities: Finalizing project closure, accomplishing administrative duties, and storing project paperwork.

5. **Post-project support and maintenance:**

- Transition: Ensuring a seamless transfer of responsibilities to operations or maintenance teams.
- Bug Fixes and Updates: Resolving any identified issues or bugs that arise after the deployment process.
- User Support: Offering continuous assistance and instruction to users as required.

Efficient software project management guarantees the timely, cost-effective, and high-quality completion of projects, satisfying the expectations of stakeholders and achieving corporate goals. Every one of these tasks is essential in attaining these objectives and providing effective software solutions.

1.4 Plans, Methods and Methodologies

In software project management, plans, methods, and methodologies are crucial components that ensure projects are executed effectively and efficiently. Here's a breakdown of each:

Plans

Plans in software project management outline the strategy and approach for achieving project goals. They typically include:

1. Project Plan: A comprehensive document that defines the scope, objectives, timeline, resources, and deliverables of the project.
2. Resource Plan: Details the human, financial, and material resources required for the project.
3. Risk Management Plan: Identifies potential risks, their impacts, and mitigation strategies.
4. Communication Plan: Outlines how information will be communicated among stakeholders.
5. Quality Assurance Plan: Describes how quality standards will be maintained throughout the project.
6. Change Management Plan: Addresses how changes to scope or requirements will be managed.

Methods

Methods refer to the specific techniques or practices used to carry out activities within the project. Common methods in software project management include:

1. Agile: Emphasizes iterative development, continuous feedback, and flexibility in responding to change.
2. Waterfall: Sequential approach with distinct phases (requirements, design, implementation, testing, deployment).

3. Scrum: A subset of Agile that focuses on cross-functional teams working in short, time-boxed iterations called sprints.
4. Kanban: Visualizes workflow to manage work in progress and optimize throughput.
5. Lean: Focuses on maximizing customer value while minimizing waste.
6. DevOps: Integrates software development (Dev) with IT operations (Ops) to improve collaboration and automation.

Methodologies

Methodologies provide a framework that guides the entire software development process. They encompass principles, practices, and procedures to ensure consistency and quality. Examples include:

1. Rational Unified Process (RUP): A structured approach that defines roles, activities, and artifacts for each phase of development.
2. Capability Maturity Model Integration (CMMI): Provides guidelines for improving processes across a project, department, or organization.
3. PRINCE2 (Projects in Controlled Environments): A structured project management method covering governance, management, and controls.
4. Extreme Programming (XP): A lightweight Agile methodology focusing on software development practices like pair programming and continuous integration.
5. Feature-Driven Development (FDD): Emphasizes designing and building features iteratively based on their priority.
6. Scaled Agile Framework (SAFe): Scales Agile practices across large organizations.

Choosing the Right Approach

The choice of plans, methods, and methodologies depends on factors such as project size, complexity, timeline, team expertise, and organizational culture. Agile methods are popular for their flexibility and responsiveness, while traditional waterfall methods suit projects with well-defined requirements and stable scope.

Successful software project management involves tailoring these plans, methods, and methodologies to fit the specific needs of each project while ensuring alignment with organizational goals and stakeholder expectations.

1.5 Management

Management in software project management encompasses a wide range of activities and responsibilities aimed at ensuring the successful planning, execution, monitoring, and completion of software projects. Here are some key aspects of management in software project management:

1. **Project Planning:**
    - **Scope Definition:** Clearly defining the goals, deliverables, features, and boundaries of the project.
    - **Resource Planning:** Allocating human, material, and financial resources effectively.
    - **Time Planning:** Creating schedules, timelines, and milestones for project activities.
2. **Risk Management:**
    - Identifying potential risks and uncertainties that could impact the project.
    - Developing strategies to mitigate risks and minimize their impact.
    - Continuously monitoring and evaluating risks throughout the project lifecycle.
3. **Communication Management:**
    - Establishing effective communication channels and protocols among team members, stakeholders, and clients.
    - Ensuring clear and timely dissemination of information, progress updates, and decisions.
4. **Quality Management:**
    - Defining quality standards and metrics for the software product.
    - Implementing processes and procedures to ensure adherence to quality standards.
    - Conducting quality assurance activities such as testing, reviews, and audits.
5. **Budget Management:**
    - Estimating and managing costs associated with the project.
    - Tracking expenses, managing budgets, and controlling expenditures.
6. **Change Management:**
    - Handling changes in project scope, requirements, or objectives.
    - Assessing the impact of changes and implementing appropriate adjustments.
    - Maintaining documentation and communication related to change requests.

7. **Team Management:**

    - Building and managing a competent project team.
    - Assigning roles and responsibilities.
    - Motivating team members, resolving conflicts, and fostering collaboration.

8. **Stakeholder Management:**

    - Identifying stakeholders and understanding their interests and expectations.
    - Engaging stakeholders throughout the project lifecycle.
    - Managing stakeholder communications and addressing concerns.

9. **Monitoring and Reporting:**

    - Monitoring project progress against plans and schedules.
    - Tracking key performance indicators (KPIs) and metrics.
    - Generating regular reports for stakeholders and management.

10. **Closure and Evaluation:**

    - Formalizing project closure activities, including documentation and handover.
    - Conducting post-project reviews and evaluations.
    - Capturing lessons learned for future projects.

Effective management in software project management requires a blend of technical expertise, leadership skills, and a structured approach to handling complexity and uncertainty inherent in software development projects. It aims to ensure that projects are delivered on time, within budget, and with the expected level of quality while meeting stakeholder expectations.

1.6 Objectives

Software project management aims to achieve several key objectives to ensure the successful delivery of software projects. These objectives can be summarized as follows:

1. **Deliver on Time:** One of the primary objectives of software project management is to deliver the software product within the agreed-upon deadlines and milestones. This involves effective scheduling, time management, and adherence to project timelines.
2. **Stay within Budget:** Controlling costs and ensuring that the project does not exceed its allocated budget is crucial. This objective involves budget planning, cost estimation, monitoring expenditures, and implementing cost-effective measures.

3. **Meet Quality Standards:** Software project management aims to deliver a product that meets the specified quality standards and requirements. This includes defining quality metrics, conducting thorough testing, and implementing quality assurance processes throughout the development lifecycle.
4. **Achieve Scope Objectives:** Managing scope involves defining the project's scope clearly at the outset, controlling scope changes effectively, and ensuring that the final product aligns with the originally defined scope and requirements.
5. **Manage Risks Effectively:** Identifying potential risks, assessing their impact and likelihood, and implementing risk mitigation strategies are essential objectives. This helps minimize disruptions and ensures smoother project execution.
6. **Maintain Communication:** Effective communication is critical to project success. The objectives here include establishing clear communication channels, ensuring stakeholders are informed and involved, and resolving communication barriers promptly.
7. **Optimize Resource Allocation:** Maximizing the utilization of resources (human, financial, and technological) while minimizing wastage is another objective. This involves resource planning, allocation, and monitoring to ensure efficient project execution.
8. **Ensure Stakeholder Satisfaction:** Meeting the expectations and requirements of stakeholders, including clients, users, and sponsors, is fundamental. This objective involves understanding stakeholder needs, managing expectations, and maintaining positive relationships.
9. **Facilitate Team Collaboration:** Promoting teamwork, collaboration, and effective leadership within the project team is crucial. This objective aims to foster a productive and motivated team environment conducive to achieving project goals.
10. **Enable Continuous Improvement:** Learning from past projects, identifying areas for improvement, and applying lessons learned to future projects is essential. This objective supports ongoing refinement of project management processes and practices.

Overall, the objectives of software project management focus on delivering projects that are on time, within budget, of high quality, and meet stakeholder expectations, while effectively managing risks and resources throughout the project lifecycle.

1.7 Stakeholders

Stakeholders in software project management are individuals, groups, or organizations that have an interest in the outcome of the project. They can significantly influence or be impacted by the project's decisions, activities, and results. Identifying and effectively managing stakeholders is crucial for the success of any software project. Here are some common stakeholders in software project management:

1. **Clients or Customers:**

   The primary stakeholders who commission the project and will ultimately use or benefit from the software product.

2. **Users:**

   Individuals or groups who will directly interact with and use the software. Their needs, preferences, and feedback are crucial for defining requirements and ensuring usability.

3. **Project Sponsor:**

   The individual or group providing financial resources, support, and strategic direction for the project. They have a significant interest in the project's success.

4. **Project Manager and Team:**

   The project manager and their team are stakeholders responsible for planning, executing, and delivering the project within scope, time, and budget constraints.

5. **Development Team:**

   Engineers, programmers, testers, and other technical experts directly involved in designing, developing, and implementing the software.

6. **Management and Executives:**

   Higher-level management within the organization responsible for overseeing the project, making strategic decisions, and providing support as needed.

7. **Quality Assurance and Testing:**

   Stakeholders responsible for ensuring the software meets quality standards and performs as expected through testing and validation processes.

8. **Marketing and Sales:**

   Stakeholders who may need to understand the software's features and benefits to market and sell it effectively.

9. **Regulatory Bodies:**

   Government agencies or regulatory bodies that may have requirements or standards the software must adhere to, particularly in regulated industries.

10. **Suppliers and Partners:**

    External entities providing resources, components, or services integral to the project's success.

11. **Competitors:**

    While not traditional stakeholders, competitors can indirectly influence the project by shaping market conditions and expectations.

12. **Community and Public Interest Groups:**

    Stakeholders who may be affected by the software project's outcomes in terms of social, environmental, or ethical considerations.

Managing stakeholders involves identifying their needs and expectations, communicating effectively with them throughout the project lifecycle, and addressing their concerns to ensure their support and cooperation. This helps in aligning the project's goals with the stakeholders' interests, ultimately contributing to the project's success.

1.8 Requirement Specification

Requirement specification in software project management refers to the process of defining and documenting the needs and expectations for a software system or application. It is a critical phase that sets the foundation for the entire project, guiding development, testing, and validation activities. Here are key aspects and best practices involved in requirement specification:

1. **Gathering Requirements:**

   - **Stakeholder Identification:** Identify and involve all relevant stakeholders (users, clients, sponsors, etc.) to capture their needs and expectations.
   - **Requirement Elicitation Techniques:** Use methods such as interviews, workshops, surveys, and observations to gather requirements comprehensively.

2. **Analyzing and Documenting Requirements:**

   - **Requirements Analysis:** Analyze gathered requirements to ensure they are clear, complete, consistent, and feasible.
   - **Documenting Requirements:** Document requirements in a structured format, typically using a Requirements Specification Document (RSD) or a Requirements Management Tool. Include details like functional requirements (what the system should do) and non-functional requirements (qualities or constraints like performance, security, etc.).

3. **Prioritizing Requirements:**

   - **MoSCoW Prioritization:** Classify requirements into Must have, Should have, Could have, and won't have categories to prioritize development efforts.
   - **Criticality and Dependency:** Assess the criticality and interdependencies of requirements to manage project risks effectively.

4. **Validating Requirements:**

   - **Requirements Reviews:** Conduct reviews with stakeholders and subject matter experts to validate requirements against business objectives and user needs.
   - **Prototyping and Mockups:** Use prototypes or mockups to visualize and validate requirements early in the development process.

5. **Managing Changes to Requirements:**

   - **Change Control Process:** Establish a formal process for managing changes to requirements to prevent scope creep and maintain project focus.
   - **Impact Analysis:** Assess the impact of proposed changes on project scope, schedule, and resources before approving them.

6. **Traceability and Documentation:**

   - **Traceability Matrix:** Maintain traceability between requirements and other project artifacts (e.g., design documents, test cases) to ensure that all requirements are addressed.
   - **Version Control:** Manage versions of the requirements document to track changes and maintain a history of requirements evolution.

7. **Communication and Collaboration:**
    - **Effective Communication:** Ensure clear and consistent communication with stakeholders throughout the requirement specification process.
    - **Collaboration Tools:** Use collaboration tools and techniques to facilitate discussions, document sharing, and feedback gathering from stakeholders.
8. **Review and Sign-off:**
    - **Formal Review:** Conduct formal reviews of the requirements document with stakeholders to obtain approval and sign-off before proceeding to the next phases of the project.

By following these practices, software project teams can effectively capture, analyze, document, and manage requirements, thereby laying a solid foundation for successful software development and delivery. This process helps mitigate risks, reduce ambiguities, and ensure that the final software product meets stakeholder expectations and business objectives.

1.9 Management Control

Management control in software project management refers to the process of monitoring, evaluating, and regulating the activities and resources within a project to ensure that goals are achieved effectively and efficiently. It involves several key aspects and practices:

1. **Setting Objectives and Milestones:**
    - **Clear Goals:** Define clear project objectives, milestones, and deliverables that align with the project's overall strategic goals.
    - **SMART Criteria:** Ensure that objectives are Specific, Measurable, Achievable, Relevant, and Time-bound.
2. **Planning and Scheduling:**
    - **Project Planning:** Develop detailed plans, schedules, and resource allocations to guide project execution.
    - **Critical Path Analysis:** Identify critical tasks and dependencies to manage project timelines effectively.

3. **Monitoring Progress:**
   - **Progress Tracking:** Regularly monitor project progress against the planned schedule, budget, and scope.
   - **Key Performance Indicators (KPIs):** Define and track KPIs such as schedule variance, cost performance index, and quality metrics to assess project health.
4. **Resource Management:**
   - **Resource Allocation:** Allocate resources (human, financial, and technological) based on project requirements and priorities.
   - **Resource Utilization:** Monitor resource utilization to optimize efficiency and address any resource constraints or bottlenecks.
5. **Risk Management:**

- **Risk Identification:** Identify potential risks and uncertainties that could impact project objectives.
- **Risk Mitigation:** Develop strategies and contingency plans to mitigate risks and minimize their impact on project outcomes.

6. **Change Management:**

- **Change Control Process:** Establish a formal process for evaluating, approving, and implementing changes to project scope, schedule, or resources.
- **Impact Assessment:** Assess the impact of proposed changes on project objectives and adjust plans accordingly.

7. **Quality Assurance:**
   - **Quality Control:** Implement processes and metrics to ensure that deliverables meet quality standards and comply with requirements.
   - **Quality Reviews:** Conduct regular reviews and inspections to identify defects or deviations early in the development process.
8. **Communication and Reporting:**
   - **Stakeholder Communication:** Maintain regular communication with stakeholders to provide updates on project progress, issues, and decisions.
   - **Project Reporting:** Prepare and distribute reports that summarize project status, achievements, risks, and upcoming milestones.

9. **Compliance and Governance:**

    - **Compliance Management:** Ensure that project activities adhere to organizational policies, industry standards, and regulatory requirements.
    - **Governance Framework:** Establish a governance framework to provide oversight and ensure accountability throughout the project lifecycle.

10. **Closure and Evaluation:**

    - **Project Review:** Conduct post-project reviews to evaluate outcomes, capture lessons learned, and identify areas for improvement.
    - **Closure Activities:** Complete formal closure activities, including documentation, handover, and transition to operational support.

Effective management control in software project management involves a systematic approach to planning, monitoring, and adjusting project activities to achieve desired outcomes within constraints. It helps to mitigate risks, optimize resources, ensure quality, and maintain alignment with stakeholder expectations throughout the project lifecycle.

1.10 Management control

Management control in software project management refers to the process of overseeing and regulating various aspects of a software project to ensure that it progresses according to plan, meets its objectives, and delivers value to stakeholders. It involves a combination of planning, monitoring, and controlling activities to maintain project discipline and achieve desired outcomes. Here are key aspects of management control in software project management:

1. **Planning:**

    - **Project Definition:** Clearly define project scope, objectives, requirements, and constraints.
    - **Resource Planning:** Allocate human, financial, and technical resources appropriately.
    - **Schedule Planning:** Develop a detailed project schedule, including milestones and deadlines.

2. **Monitoring and Tracking:**

    - **Progress Monitoring:** Regularly track project activities and milestones against the planned schedule and budget.

- **Performance Metrics:** Define and measure key performance indicators (KPIs) such as schedule variance, budget variance, and quality metrics.
- **Issue Tracking:** Identify and address issues, risks, and deviations from the plan promptly.

3. **Controlling:**

- **Risk Management:** Proactively identify, assess, and manage risks throughout the project lifecycle.
- **Change Management:** Implement a formal process to evaluate, approve, and manage changes to project scope, requirements, or schedule.
- **Quality Control:** Establish processes and standards to ensure that deliverables meet quality requirements and adhere to best practices.

4. **Communication and Reporting:**

- **Stakeholder Communication:** Maintain clear and regular communication with stakeholders to keep them informed of project progress, issues, and decisions.
- **Reporting:** Prepare and distribute periodic reports that summarize project status, achievements, challenges, and upcoming activities.

5. **Resource Management:**

- **Resource Allocation:** Optimize the allocation and utilization of resources to maximize efficiency and productivity.
- **Conflict Resolution:** Address conflicts or resource constraints that may arise during project execution.

6. **Compliance and Governance:**

- **Compliance Management:** Ensure that project activities comply with organizational policies, standards, and regulatory requirements.
- **Governance Framework:** Establish governance processes and structures to provide oversight, accountability, and decision-making authority.

7. **Closure and Evaluation:**

- **Project Closure:** Complete formal closure activities, including documentation, handover, and transition to operational support.
- **Post-Project Evaluation:** Conduct a post-project review to assess outcomes, capture lessons learned, and identify opportunities for improvement in future projects.

Effective management control in software project management requires a structured approach, attention to detail, proactive problem-solving, and strong leadership. It aims to minimize risks, optimize resources, ensure quality deliverables, and ultimately achieve successful project outcomes that meet stakeholder expectations.

1.11 Activities Covered By Software Project Management

Software project management involves a wide range of activities aimed at planning, executing, monitoring, and closing software projects effectively. These activities typically encompass the following:

1. **Project Initiation:**
    - **Project Charter:** Developing a project charter that outlines the project objectives, scope, stakeholders, and initial requirements.
    - **Feasibility Study:** Assessing the feasibility of the project in terms of technical, economic, and operational aspects.
2. **Project Planning:**
    - **Scope Management:** Defining and managing the project scope, including requirements gathering and scope validation.
    - **Schedule Management:** Developing a project schedule, identifying tasks, dependencies, and milestones.
    - **Resource Management:** Allocating and managing resources (human, financial, and equipment) required for the project.
    - **Risk Management:** Identifying, assessing, and mitigating risks that could impact project objectives.
    - **Quality Management:** Planning and implementing processes to ensure the quality of deliverables meets requirements.
3. **Project Execution:**
    - **Task Execution:** Assigning tasks to team members, monitoring progress, and ensuring work is completed according to schedule and quality standards.
    - **Communication Management:** Facilitating communication among team members, stakeholders, and management to ensure everyone is informed and aligned.
    - **Change Management:** Managing changes to project scope, schedule, or resources and assessing their impact on the project.
    - **Issue Management:** Identifying and resolving issues or conflicts that arise during project execution.
4. **Monitoring and Control:**
    - **Progress Monitoring:** Tracking project progress against the planned schedule and budget, identifying variances, and taking corrective actions.

- **Quality Assurance:** Conducting reviews, inspections, and tests to verify that deliverables meet quality standards.
- **Risk Monitoring:** Continuously monitoring identified risks and implementing responses as necessary.

5. **Project Closure:**
   - **Closure Activities:** Formalizing project closure by delivering final deliverables, documenting lessons learned, and obtaining client acceptance.
   - **Post-Project Review:** Conducting a post-mortem review to evaluate project success, identify strengths and areas for improvement, and document recommendations for future projects.
6. **Stakeholder Management:**
   - **Identifying Stakeholders:** Identifying all stakeholders involved in or affected by the project and understanding their needs and expectations.
   - **Engagement:** Engaging stakeholders throughout the project lifecycle to gather requirements, provide updates, and manage expectations.
7. **Documentation and Reporting:**
   - **Project Documentation:** Maintaining accurate and comprehensive documentation throughout the project, including requirements documents, design documents, and test plans.
   - **Reporting:** Providing regular progress reports to stakeholders and management, including status updates, issues, risks, and milestone achievements.
8. **Team Management:**
   - **Team Building:** Building and maintaining an effective project team, assigning roles and responsibilities, and fostering collaboration and communication.
   - **Motivation and Conflict Resolution:** Motivating team members, resolving conflicts, and ensuring a positive team environment conducive to productivity and creativity.

These activities are interrelated and iterative, often overlapping throughout the project lifecycle. Effective software project management requires careful planning, diligent execution, proactive monitoring, and adaptive control to ensure successful project outcomes within scope, schedule, budget, and quality constraints.

1.12 Overview of Project Planning

Project planning in software project management is a crucial phase that sets the foundation for a successful project execution. It involves defining project goals, scope, tasks, resources, timelines, and deliverables. Here's an overview of the key aspects of project planning in software project management:

1. **Defining Project Objectives:**
    - **Purpose and Goals:** Clearly articulate the objectives of the project, including what needs to be achieved and why it's important to stakeholders.
    - **SMART Criteria:** Ensure objectives are Specific, Measurable, Achievable, Relevant, and Time-bound to provide clarity and focus.
2. **Project Scope Definition:**
    - **Scope Statement:** Document the boundaries, deliverables, features, and constraints of the project.
    - **Scope Verification:** Validate the scope with stakeholders to ensure agreement on what will be included and excluded from the project.
3. **Creating Work Breakdown Structure (WBS):**
    - **Decomposing Tasks:** Break down project deliverables into smaller, manageable tasks and activities.
    - **Organizing Hierarchically:** Structure the WBS in a hierarchical format to show how tasks roll up to deliverables and project phases.
4. **Estimating Resources:**
    - **Resource Identification:** Identify human, financial, equipment, and material resources required for each task.
    - **Resource Allocation:** Allocate resources based on availability, skill sets, and project requirements.
5. **Developing a Project Schedule:**
    - **Task Sequencing:** Sequence tasks logically to define dependencies and the order of execution.
    - **Critical Path Analysis:** Identify the critical path—the sequence of tasks that determines the project's duration.
    - **Gantt Chart:** Create a visual representation of the project schedule using a Gantt chart to illustrate task timelines and dependencies.
6. **Risk Management Planning:**
    - **Risk Identification:** Identify potential risks that could impact project objectives.
    - **Risk Assessment:** Evaluate the likelihood and impact of identified risks.
    - **Risk Response Planning:** Develop strategies to mitigate, avoid, transfer, or accept risks.
7. **Quality Planning:**
    - **Quality Standards:** Define quality criteria and metrics that will be used to measure the project's deliverables.
    - **Quality Assurance:** Plan processes and activities to ensure that quality standards are met throughout the project lifecycle.
8. **Communication Planning:**
    - **Stakeholder Communication:** Identify stakeholders, determine their information needs, and plan communication channels and frequency.

- **Communication Management Plan:** Document how communication will be managed, including protocols for meetings, reports, and updates.

9. **Procurement Planning (if applicable):**
    - **Procurement Strategy:** Determine if external resources or services are needed and plan for their procurement.
    - **Vendor Selection:** Identify potential vendors, solicit bids or proposals, and select vendors based on criteria such as cost, capability, and reliability.
10. **Change Management Planning:**
    - **Change Control Process:** Establish procedures for managing changes to project scope, schedule, or resources.
    - **Change Impact Assessment:** Assess the impact of proposed changes on project objectives and adjust plans accordingly.
11. **Contingency Planning:**
    - **Risk Response Plans:** Develop contingency plans for identified risks to minimize their impact on project outcomes.
    - **Alternative Strategies:** Identify alternative approaches or plans in case initial assumptions or conditions change.

Project planning in software project management requires thorough analysis, collaboration with stakeholders, and meticulous documentation to ensure all aspects of the project are adequately planned for and managed. It sets the stage for efficient execution and facilitates proactive management throughout the project lifecycle.

1.13 Stepwise Project Planning

Stepwise project planning in software project management involves a structured approach to defining, organizing, and documenting the project's objectives, scope, tasks, resources, schedule, and deliverables. Here is a step-by-step guide to project planning in software project management:

1. **Define Project Objectives and Scope:**
    - **Objective Definition:** Clearly articulate the project's goals, outcomes, and objectives. Use the SMART criteria (Specific, Measurable, Achievable, Relevant, and Time-bound) to ensure clarity.
    - **Scope Definition:** Define the boundaries of the project, including what will be included (in-scope) and excluded (out-of-scope). Document any constraints and assumptions.
2. **Identify Stakeholders and Gather Requirements:**
    - **Stakeholder Identification:** Identify all stakeholders involved or affected by the project, including clients, users, sponsors, and team members.

- **Requirements Gathering:** Engage with stakeholders to gather and document functional and non-functional requirements. Use techniques such as interviews, workshops, and surveys.

3. **Create a Work Breakdown Structure (WBS):**
   - **Decompose Deliverables:** Break down project deliverables into smaller, manageable components or tasks.
   - **Hierarchical Structure:** Organize tasks in a hierarchical format to illustrate how they relate to each other and to project phases.
4. **Estimate Resources:**
   - **Resource Identification:** Identify human resources (skills and roles needed), equipment, materials, and budgetary requirements.
   - **Resource Allocation:** Allocate resources based on availability, skills, and project needs. Consider resource constraints and dependencies.
5. **Develop a Project Schedule:**
   - **Task Sequencing:** Sequence tasks based on dependencies and logical order of execution. Identify critical path tasks that determine the project's duration.
   - **Gantt Chart:** Create a Gantt chart or similar visual representation to depict task timelines, dependencies, and milestones.
6. **Risk Management Planning:**
   - **Risk Identification:** Identify potential risks that could impact project objectives, schedule, or quality.
   - **Risk Assessment:** Assess the likelihood and impact of identified risks. Prioritize risks based on severity.
   - **Risk Response Planning:** Develop strategies to mitigate, avoid, transfer, or accept risks. Assign responsibilities for risk management tasks.
7. **Quality Planning:**
   - **Quality Standards:** Define quality criteria and metrics that will be used to evaluate project deliverables.
   - **Quality Assurance:** Plan for processes, reviews, and activities to ensure that quality standards are met throughout the project lifecycle.
8. **Communication Planning:**
   - **Stakeholder Communication:** Determine communication needs and preferences of stakeholders. Define communication channels, frequency, and protocols.
   - **Communication Management Plan:** Document how information will be communicated, including reporting formats, meeting schedules, and escalation procedures.
9. **Procurement Planning (if applicable):**
   - **Procurement Strategy:** Determine if external products, services, or resources are needed. Define procurement requirements and selection criteria.

- **Vendor Management:** Identify potential vendors or suppliers, solicit bids or proposals, and select vendors based on cost, capability, and suitability.

10. **Change Management Planning:**
    - **Change Control Process:** Establish procedures for requesting, evaluating, approving, and implementing changes to project scope, schedule, or resources.
    - **Change Impact Assessment:** Assess the potential impact of proposed changes on project objectives, schedule, budget, and quality.
11. **Contingency Planning:**
    - **Risk Response Plans:** Develop contingency plans for high-priority risks to minimize their impact on project outcomes.
    - **Alternative Strategies:** Identify alternative approaches or plans in case initial assumptions or conditions change unexpectedly.
12. **Document the Project Plan:**
    - **Project Management Plan:** Compile all planning documentation into a comprehensive Project Management Plan (PMP). Ensure the PMP is accessible to all project stakeholders and serves as a reference throughout the project lifecycle.

By following these steps, software project managers can systematically plan and organize their projects, ensuring clarity, alignment with stakeholder expectations, and effective management of resources, risks, and changes. This structured approach lays the groundwork for successful project execution and delivery.

Chapter 2

PROJECT EVALUATION

Project assessment is a structured approach that involves gathering, examining, and utilizing data to address inquiries regarding the performance and productivity of projects, policies, and programs. Project evaluation is a comprehensive examination of the project's viability and potential, determining whether it is advisable to continue with the project.

To determine if the project aligns with the overall strategic planning of the business, project evaluation is typically conducted during the initial phase of a stepwise process.

Project evaluation is a systematic procedure that involves gathering, documenting, and arranging data pertaining to the outcomes of a project.

- Short-term outputs refer to the immediate results of operations or project deliverables.

- Long-term outcomes (alterations in behavior, practices, or policies as a consequence of the outcome).

The significance of project evaluation is in its ability to assess the effectiveness and efficiency of a project, providing valuable insights into its outcomes, impacts, and overall success.

Project evaluation is crucial for addressing the following inquiries. What advancements have been achieved?

Were the intended results accomplished? For what reason?

- Can the project be improved to generate more favorable results?

Do the outcomes of the project validate the resources invested in the project?

Project evaluation is utilized to determine whether a project can progress in a timely manner. It is also employed to determine which of multiple potential projects has a higher likelihood of success, a greater turnover, and other favorable outcomes.

Is it advantageous to undertake the development and operation of the software system?

Project evaluation is conducted by senior management, the project manager/coordinator, and the team leader.

Project evaluation includes a strategic assessment, a technical assessment, and an economic review.

Strategic planning

Strategic planning refers to the systematic process by which an organization determines its overall strategy and makes decisions regarding the allocation of its resources, such as capital and personnel, to achieve this strategy.

- What actions should we take?

- Who is the recipient of our actions?

- How can we achieve excellence?

2.1 Strategic Assessment

Strategic assessment in software project management entails the careful evaluation of many factors to ensure that they are in line with the overall aims of the organization and to achieve successful outcomes for the project. The following are the primary areas that are normally taken into consideration:

1. Project's objectives: Evaluate the clarity and alignment of the project's objectives with the strategic goals of the organization. This entails comprehending the project's contribution to business objectives, market positioning, or customer requirements.

2. Risk Assessment: Identify and assess any risks that may have an impact on the project's success. This encompasses technical risks, such as the intricacy of the technological stack, commercial risks, such as fluctuations in market demand, and operational risks, such as limitations in resources.

3. Resource Planning involves evaluating the accessibility and distribution of the necessary resources for the project, such as staff, finances, infrastructure, and tools. Ensure that the allocation of resources is in accordance with the specified project schedules and requirements.

4. Conduct a stakeholder analysis to assess the interests, expectations, and level of influence that stakeholders have on the project. Identify and evaluate the demands of key stakeholders, including clients, users, management, and the development team, in order to effectively manage expectations and maintain effective communication.

5. Technology and Architecture Review: Evaluate the appropriateness of selected technologies and architecture in satisfying project requirements and scalability. Assess several options and make sure they are in line with the organization's long-term IT plans and guidelines.

6. Conduct a feasibility study to evaluate if the project can be effectively accomplished within the limitations of time, budget, and resources. Detect any possible obstacles or issues at an early stage of the planning process.

7. Conduct a market and competitive analysis to gain a comprehensive understanding of the project's market landscape and competitive environment. Evaluate how the project may establish a competitive edge or effectively meet market demands in comparison to current options.

8. Conduct a cost-benefit analysis to assess the expected expenses and advantages of the project. This encompasses not only the financial factors but also qualitative advantages such as enhanced customer happiness, operational effectiveness, or strategic positioning.

9. Performance Metrics and KPIs: Establish and articulate the essential performance indicators (KPIs) and metrics to evaluate and quantify the advancement and achievement of the project. This enables continuous evaluation and modification of project strategies using up-to-date data.

10. Change Management Strategy: Formulate a comprehensive plan for effectively handling modifications at every stage of the project's lifespan. Foresee possible alterations in requirements, scope, or priorities, and strategize how they will be assessed, authorized, and executed.

Through a comprehensive strategic evaluation in these domains, software project managers may more effectively predict obstacles, exploit advantages, and synchronize project tasks with corporate strategies to achieve successful results.

2.1.1 Programme management

D.C. Ferns defined "a programme as a group of projects that are managed in a coordinated way to gain benefits that would not be possible were the projects to be managed independently".

• A programme in this context is a "collection of projects that all contribute to the sameoverall organization goals".

• Effective programme management requires that there is a well defined programme goal and that all the organization's projects are selected and tuned to contribute to this goal"

Evaluating of project is depends on:

• How it contributes to programme goal.

• It is viability [capability of developing or useful].

• Timing.

• Resourcing.

For successful strategic assessment, there should be a strategic plan which defines:

• Organization's objectives.

• Provides context for defining programme .

• Provides context for defining programme goals.

• Provide context for accessing individual project.

In large organization, programme management is taken care by programme director and programme executive, rather than, project manager, who will be responsible for the strategic assessment of project. Any potential software system will form part of the user organization's overall information system and must be evaluated within the context of existing information system and the organization's information strategy. If a well – defined information system does not exist then the system development and the assessment of project proposals will be based on a more "piece meal approach". Piece meal approach is one in which each project being individually early in its life cycle

2.1.2 Typical issues and questions to be considered during strategic assessment

Issue – 1: objectives:

– How will the proposed system contribute to the organization's stated objectives? How, for example, might it contribute to an increase in market share?

Issue – 2: is plan

How does the proposed system fit in to the IS plan? Which existing system (s) will it replace/interface with? How will it interact with systems proposed for the later development?

Issue – 3: organization structure:

– What effect will the new system have on the existing departmental and organization structure?

– For example, a new sales order processing system overlap existing sales andstock control functions?

Issue – 4: MIS:

– What information will the system provide and at what levels in the organization? In what ways will it complement or enhance existing management information system?

Issue – 5: personnel:

– In what way will the system proposed system affect manning levels and the existing employee skill base? What are the implications for the organization's overall policy on staff development.

Issue – 6: image:

– What, if any, will be the effect on customer's attitudes towards the organization? Will the adoption of, say, automated system conflict with the objectives of providing a friendly service?

2.1.3 Portfolio management

Project Portfolio management provides an overview of all the projects that an organization is undertaking or is considering. It prioritizes the allocation of resources to projects and decides which projects should be accepted and which existing ones should be dropped.

The concerns of Project Portfolio management include:

- Identifying which project proposals are worth implementation;
- Assessing the amount of risk of failure that a potential project has;
- Deciding how to share limited resources, including staff time and finance, between projects;
- Being aware of the dependencies between projects;
- Ensuring that projects do not duplicate benefits;
- Ensuring that necessary developments have been inadvertently been missed.

The three key aspects of Project Portfolio management are:

1. Portfolio definition

2. Portfolio management

3. Portfolio optimization

2.2 Technical Assessment

Technical assessment is the second criteria for evaluating the project.

Technical assessment of a proposed system evaluates functionality against available:

• Hardware

• Software

• Limitations

– Nature of solutions produced by strategic information systems plan

– Cost of solution. Hence undergoes cost-benefit analysis.

It is also referred as Technology Evaluation. The Technology Assessment is a writeup on the technical aspects of the project sector and planned technical purchases.

Technology is defined broadly here to include: equipment, tools, products, processes, raw materials, skills, and ways of organizing production.

Assessing Technology Planning:

- Analyze Technology Needs

- Planning for Change and Technology

- Assessing a Technology Plan Before and After Implementation

Why it is important:

- It's a tool to Identify the Problem
- At the core of any project is a series of big and small problems that need to be addressed (ex: not enough production capacity, staff lacks required skills, overly expensive transportation, etc.)
- Reviewing the production process including the systems and equipment in place
- Provides transparency into what some of the constraints are. Some will be obvious, but others may be hidden until you take a closer look.
- Not all constraints will be technical, so this is just one investigative tool needed.
- It's a tool to Identify the Best Solution
- Once you know what the technical problems are, you can start to look for solutions.
- The Technology Assessment provides the opportunity to explore potential solutions

(Ex: new equipment choices, new crop varieties, new fertilizers, changes in process,

etc.)

The grantee often has a solution in mind when they propose the project, but further analysis can lead to more creative, better fitting, and more cost effective solutions. The grant budget is limited, so looking at the options in a systematic way helps the grantee understand the tradeoffs with implementing one technical solution or another. Knowing this, they can make more informed decisions about using scarce budget resources.

It's a tool for Communication

The write-up documents the background work and thinking on technical issues that has gone into the project design and budget.

(1) The more people understand the logic of the proposal, the more they can help brainstorm on solutions or help catch problems that might not have been fully addressed.

(2) A clear presentation will reduce questions from ADFW on the project proposal and will help them better understand the design choices despite not being present for all of the partner discussions with the grantee.

o It serves as a record and resource for the grantee in case they need to go back and reconsider the options at a later date.

Purpose:

- Technology assessment provides an organization with information about the profitability of current technology as well as the benefits of implementing new technology.

- Ineffective technology needs to be upgraded or replaced for businesses to produce quality products or services.

Types of Assessments:

Technology assessment can happen on several levels: flexibility, longevity and upgrade and scale-assessments. To assure that an organization can remain competitive, every aspect of its technology system must be in excellent operating condition. Assessment on all four levels improves the chances of this happening.

- Flexibility/Longevity

Flexibility assessment examines how technology will adapt to new levels of applications and other technology systems. Longevity assessment provides information on how long the technology will last.

- Upgrade/Scale Assessments

An upgrade assessment determines the ability of the technology to function with the addition of new, advanced features and equipment. Scale assessment considers how well the technology can operate in a larger, ever-growing network of systems. The growth of an organization means developing larger technology system. New technology must be able to be incorporated into new, expanding networks.

Evaluate the technology options on the following factors:

- Fixed capital costs
- Source of equipment
- Operation, maintenance, and replacement costs
- Scale of production and expected capacity use rate

- Reliability
- Labor intensiveness (labor costs, productivity, and employment generation)
- Types and amounts of inputs required
- Raw material availability, sustainability, and cost
- Effects on product quality, cost and marketability
- Foreign exchange requirements and availability
- Natural resource requirements and sustainability
- Compatibility with existing technology in use
- Human resource requirement (training and technical assistance costs, management and
- supervision costs, etc)

2.3 Cost Benefit Analysis

Cost-benefit analysis (CBA) in software project management is a critical process used to evaluate the financial and non-financial costs and benefits associated with a project. It helps project managers and stakeholders make informed decisions about whether to proceed with a project, which alternatives to choose, or whether to make adjustments to the project scope or approach. Here's how CBA is applied in software project management:

Steps in Cost-Benefit Analysis:

1. **Identify Costs and Benefits:**

    - **Costs:** These include direct costs (e.g., software development, hardware, licensing), indirect costs (e.g., training, maintenance, support), and opportunity costs (e.g., potential revenue from alternative projects).
    - **Benefits:** These encompass direct benefits (e.g., revenue generation, cost savings from process automation), indirect benefits (e.g., improved customer satisfaction, enhanced brand reputation), and intangible benefits (e.g., increased innovation, reduced risk).

2. **Quantify Costs and Benefits:**

    - Assign monetary values to both costs and benefits where possible. Direct costs are usually easier to quantify (e.g., development hours multiplied by hourly rates), while indirect and intangible costs may require more estimation or qualitative assessment.
    - Benefits may be quantified through projected revenue increases, cost reductions, or efficiency gains. For intangible benefits, stakeholders' perceptions or industry benchmarks may be used.

3. **Estimate Timeframes:**

    - Define the timeframe over which costs and benefits will be assessed. In software projects, this may cover development, implementation, and ongoing maintenance phases, along with expected benefits realization periods.

4. **Calculate Net Present Value (NPV):**

    - Adjust future costs and benefits to their present value using a discount rate to account for the time value of money. NPV calculates whether the project is financially viable by comparing the present value of expected benefits to the present value of expected costs.

5. **Perform Sensitivity Analysis:**

    - Assess the impact of uncertainties or variations in key assumptions (e.g., project duration, market demand) on the project's financial outcomes. Sensitivity analysis helps identify which factors have the greatest influence on the project's cost-benefit ratio.

6. **Consider Non-Financial Factors:**

    - While financial metrics are crucial, consider non-financial factors such as strategic alignment, competitive advantage, risk reduction, and compliance requirements. These factors contribute to the overall decision-making process alongside financial considerations.

7. **Make Informed Decisions:**

    - Based on the analysis, stakeholders can decide whether to proceed with the project, adjust its scope or approach, or explore alternative solutions that offer a better cost-benefit ratio.

Benefits of Cost-Benefit Analysis in Software Project Management:

- **Decision Support:** Helps stakeholders objectively evaluate project proposals and make informed decisions based on quantifiable data.
- **Risk Assessment:** Identifies potential risks and uncertainties associated with the project's financial outcomes.

- **Resource Allocation:** Guides allocation of resources (e.g., budget, personnel) to maximize return on investment and minimize costs.
- **Performance Evaluation:** Provides a basis for monitoring and evaluating project performance against initial projections and adjusting strategies as needed.

In conclusion, cost-benefit analysis plays a crucial role in software project management by providing a structured approach to assessing financial viability, evaluating alternatives, and optimizing resource allocation to achieve desired project outcomes.

2.4 Cash Flow Forecasting

When managing a software project, it's important to make a cash flow forecast to keep the finances stable and make good decisions about how to use resources. A organized way to make a cash flow forecast for a software project is shown below:

1. Figure out the project's stages and schedule

    - Beginning: Figure out when the job will begin and end.
    - Execution: Split the project into stages, such as gathering specifications, designing, developing, testing, and deploying.

2. Guess the costs

    - Costs directly: List the costs that are directly connected to the project, such as the salaries of team members, the cost of software licenses, and the cost of hardware.
    - Indirect Costs: These are things like office rent, utilities, and management costs.

3. Estimate money or income

    - Decide how the project will be paid for (for example, through client payments, loans, or money from within the company).
    - Guess when money or income will start coming in.

4. Make a timeline of your cash flow

    - Make a schedule of when you will get cash and when you need to pay your bills.
    - Split it up into weekly or monthly payments, based on how long the project takes and when the payments are due.

5. Think about how the project depends on other projects

    - Think about the things that could affect your cash flow, like milestone payouts, late invoices, and unexpected costs.

6. Plan for what could go wrong

- Add a cushion for costs or delays that come up out of the blue that could affect cash flow.

7. Keep an eye on and update every time

- Update the cash flow forecast often based on real income and expenses.
- Track and handle cash flow with accounting tools or spreadsheets.

Steps for Example:

- Months 1-2: Start-up phase (costs of setting up and hiring people).
- Months 3 through 6: The execution step (costs of development, software licenses).
- Weeks 7 and 8: Testing and quality control process.
- Month 9: Deployment and completion (training and help for clients).

Computer and tool sets:

- Spreadsheet Tools: You can use Excel and Google Sheets to make and change cash flow predictions.
- For automatic tracking and planning, accounting software like QuickBooks and Xero are great choices.
- Software for managing projects: Jira and Trello are two examples of tools that may have built-in financial tracking features.

Good things:

Planning your finances helps you deal with cash flow problems and makes sure you have money when you need it.

Risk management finds possible financial risks and lets people take steps to reduce them.

Decision-Making: Gives information for making smart choices based on expected financial health.

In software project management, making a cash flow model requires careful planning and regular review. It makes sure that the project can stay financially successful throughout its entire lifecycle and helps make good use of resources. Project managers can deal with money problems and get the best results from their projects by following a structured method and using the right tools.

2.5 Cost Benefit Evaluation Techniques

Cost-benefit evaluation techniques are crucial in software project management to assess the financial feasibility and overall value of proposed projects or initiatives. Here are some commonly used techniques:

1. **Return on Investment (ROI):**
    - **Definition:** ROI calculates the financial return from an investment relative to its cost.
    - **Formula:** ROI=Net BenefitCost×100%ROI = \frac{Net\ Benefit}{Cost} \times 100\%ROI=CostNet Benefit×100%
    - **Application:** Used to compare potential projects and prioritize those with higher ROI.
2. **Net Present Value (NPV):**
    - **Definition:** NPV evaluates the profitability of a project by discounting all expected future cash flows to their present value, considering the time value of money.
    - **Formula:** NPV=∑(1+r)t Net Benefit$_t$ Cost

      Where r is the discount rate,

      t is the time period, and Net Benefit Cost is the net benefit in each period.

    - **Application:** Projects with positive NPV are generally considered financially viable.
3. **Cost-Benefit Analysis (CBA):**
    - **Definition:** CBA compares the total expected costs of a project against its total expected benefits to determine whether the benefits outweigh the costs.
    - **Application:** Provides a structured approach to decision-making by quantifying both tangible and intangible costs and benefits.
4. **Payback Period:**
    - **Definition:** Payback period calculates the time it takes for an investment to generate sufficient cash flows to cover its initial cost.
    - **Formula:** Identify the time it takes for an investment to pay for itself.
    - **Application:** Useful for assessing risk and liquidity by determining how quickly an investment can recover its initial cost.
5. **Benefit-Cost Ratio (BCR):**
    - **Definition:** BCR compares the total expected benefits of a project to its total expected costs.
    - **Formula:** BCR=Total Benefits Total Costs BCR = \ frac {Total\ Benefits}{Total\ Costs}BCR=Total Costs Total Benefits
    - **Application:** Helps in ranking projects based on their cost-effectiveness; projects with BCR > 1 are generally considered beneficial.
6. **Opportunity Cost Analysis:**
    - **Definition:** Evaluates the potential benefits of a project against the potential benefits of alternative uses of resources (opportunity costs).

- **Application:** Helps in assessing trade-offs and making decisions that maximize overall benefit.

7. **Risk Assessment and Contingency Planning:**
    - **Definition:** Evaluates potential risks associated with the project and identifies strategies to mitigate them.
    - **Application:** Ensures that potential losses or setbacks are accounted for in the cost-benefit analysis.

These techniques can be used individually or in combination depending on the complexity and specific requirements of the software project. They help project managers and stakeholders make informed decisions about project selection, resource allocation, and risk management.

2.5.1 Net Profit

Net Profit is a crucial evaluation technique in software project management, providing insight into the financial performance and viability of a project. Here's a detailed look at its relevance, calculation, and application within software projects.

Importance of Net Profit in Software Projects

1. **Financial Viability**: Indicates whether the project is generating sufficient returns compared to costs.
2. **Investment Decisions**: Assists stakeholders in deciding whether to continue, pivot, or terminate a project based on profitability.
3. **Resource Allocation**: Helps in determining how resources should be allocated among different projects based on their profitability.
4. **Performance Benchmarking**: Provides a metric for comparing different projects or product lines within the organization.

Calculating Net Profit for Software Projects

The formula for calculating Net Profit in the context of software projects remains the same:

Net Profit=Total Revenue−Total Expenses

Where:

- **Total Revenue**: Revenue generated from software sales, subscriptions, licensing, maintenance, and support services.
- **Total Expenses**: All costs incurred during the project lifecycle, which can include:
    - **Development Costs**: Salaries of developers, tools, and technology costs.
    - **Operational Costs**: Infrastructure, hosting, and software maintenance.

- **Marketing Costs**: Advertising, promotional expenses, and sales costs.
- **Administrative Costs**: Overhead and general administrative expenses.

Example Calculation

Scenario: A software company launches a new application.

1. **Total Revenue**: $1,000,000
2. **Total Expenses**:
   - Development Costs: $400,000
   - Operational Costs: $200,000
   - Marketing Costs: $150,000
   - Administrative Costs: $100,000

$$\text{Total Expenses}=400{,}000+200{,}000+150{,}000+100{,}000=850{,}000$$

$$\text{Net Profit}=1{,}000{,}000-850{,}000=150{,}000$$

Evaluating Net Profit in Software Projects

1. **Net Profit Margin**:

   $$\text{Net Profit Margin}=(\text{Net Profit} / \text{Total Revenue})\times 100$$

   This shows the percentage of revenue that translates into profit, providing insight into operational efficiency.

2. **ROI (Return on Investment)**:

   $$\text{ROI}=(\text{Net Profit} / \text{Total Costs})\times 100$$

   Measures the profitability of the investment made in the software project.

3. **Comparison Across Projects**: Analyzing net profit across multiple software projects can help identify which projects yield the best financial returns.

2.5.2 Payback Period

The payback period is a financial metric that calculates the time required to recover the initial investment in a project. It indicates how long it will take for a project to generate enough cash flow to cover its initial costs.

Importance:

- Helps assess the risk associated with an investment.
- Aids decision-making by providing a straightforward metric for comparison.
- Useful for determining project viability in terms of cash flow.

Calculation of Payback Period

1. **Identify Initial Investment:**
    - Total costs associated with the project (e.g., development, infrastructure, licensing).
2. **Estimate Cash Flows:**
    - Forecast the expected cash inflows generated by the project over time (monthly, quarterly, or annually).
3. **Calculate Payback Period:**
    - The payback period can be calculated using the formula:

$$\text{Payback Period} = \text{Initial Investment} \div \text{Annual Cash Inflow}$$

If cash inflows vary, sum the cash inflows until they equal the initial investment.

Example

- **Initial Investment:** $100,000
- **Yearly Cash Inflow:**
    - Year 1: $30,000
    - Year 2: $40,000
    - Year 3: $50,000

Cumulative Cash Flows:

- End of Year 1: $30,000
- End of Year 2: $70,000
- End of Year 3: $120,000

Payback Period Calculation:

- By the end of Year 2, $70,000 has been recovered. In Year 3, it takes an additional:

$$\text{Remaining} = 100{,}000 - 70{,}000 = 30{,}000$$

Since Year 3 cash inflow is $50,000, the payback occurs sometime during Year 3.

Pros and Cons

Pros:

- **Simplicity:** Easy to calculate and understand.
- **Risk Assessment:** Helps identify high-risk projects that take longer to pay back.
- **Short-term Focus:** Prioritizes projects with quicker returns.

Cons:

- **Ignores Time Value of Money:** Doesn't account for the present value of future cash flows.
- **No Profitability Insight:** Does not measure overall profitability beyond the payback period.
- **Short-term Focus:** Can lead to the neglect of long-term benefits.

Applications in Software Project Management

1. **Project Evaluation:** Use the payback period to compare multiple software projects and prioritize those with shorter payback times.
2. **Budgeting:** Helps in determining if a project aligns with the organization's cash flow requirements.
3. **Investment Decision:** Useful for stakeholders when deciding whether to proceed with development.

2.5.3 Return on Investment (ROI)

Return on Investment (ROI) is a financial metric used to evaluate the profitability of an investment relative to its cost. It measures the efficiency of an investment and helps stakeholders understand the value generated from a project.

Formula: The ROI can be calculated using the formula:

ROI=(Cost of Investment / Net Profit) ×100

Where:

- **Net Profit** = Total Revenue - Total Costs

Importance of ROI in Software Project Management

1. **Investment Justification:** Helps justify the investment in software projects to stakeholders and decision-makers.
2. **Comparative Analysis:** Facilitates comparison between multiple projects or investments, aiding in prioritization.
3. **Performance Measurement:** Provides a metric to evaluate project success after implementation.

Calculating ROI

1. **Identify Costs:**
   - **Initial Investment:** Development costs, software licenses, hardware, and training.
   - **Ongoing Costs:** Maintenance, support, and operational costs.
2. **Estimate Benefits:**
   - **Revenue Increases:** Additional sales or revenue generated directly from the software.
   - **Cost Savings:** Efficiency gains, reduced labor costs, and decreased operational expenses.
3. **Calculate Net Profit:**
   - Subtract the total costs from the total benefits.

Example Calculation

Assumptions:

- **Initial Investment:** $200,000
- **Ongoing Costs (3 years):** $50,000/year = $150,000
- **Total Revenue Generated Over 3 Years:** $500,000

Total Costs:

Total Costs=Initial Investment+Ongoing Costs=200,000+150,000=350,000

Net Profit:

Net Profit=Total Revenue−Total Costs=500,000−350,000=150,000

ROI Calculation:

$\text{ROI}= (150{,}000/350{,}000)\times 100 \approx 42.86\%$

Pros and Cons of ROI

Pros:

- **Clear Indicator:** Provides a straightforward measure of profitability.
- **Easy Comparison:** Allows for easy comparison between different projects or investments.
- **Decision-Making Support:** Aids in making informed investment decisions.

Cons:

- **Time Frame Ignorance:** Does not account for the time value of money unless adjusted.
- **Intangible Benefits:** May overlook non-monetary benefits such as customer satisfaction or market positioning.
- **Short-Term Focus:** Can encourage short-term thinking rather than long-term strategic goals.

Applications in Software Project Management

1. **Project Selection:** Use ROI to evaluate and select projects that align with business goals and provide the best returns.
2. **Performance Tracking:** Monitor ROI during and after project implementation to assess ongoing value.
3. **Stakeholder Communication:** Present ROI to stakeholders to demonstrate project value and secure ongoing support.

2.5.4 Net Present Value (NPV)

Net Present Value (NPV) is a financial metric that assesses the profitability of an investment by calculating the difference between the present value of cash inflows and the present value of cash outflows over a project's lifetime.

Formula:

$$\text{NPV} - \sum \left(\frac{C_t}{(1+r)^t} \right) - C_0$$

Where:

- C_t = Cash inflow during the period t

- r = Discount rate (cost of capital)
- t= Time period
- C_o = Initial investment

Importance of NPV in Software Project Management

1. **Investment Evaluation:** Helps determine whether a project will generate value over its lifespan.
2. **Risk Assessment:** Provides insight into the financial risks associated with a project by incorporating the time value of money.
3. **Comparison Tool:** Facilitates comparison between different projects, guiding decision-making based on expected profitability.

Calculating NPV

1. **Identify Cash Flows:**
    - Estimate the expected cash inflows generated by the project for each period (yearly, quarterly).
    - Include initial investment as a cash outflow.
2. **Select a Discount Rate:**
    - Determine an appropriate discount rate, often the organization's required rate of return or cost of capital.
3. **Calculate Present Values:**
    - Discount future cash flows back to their present value using the formula.
4. **Sum Cash Flows:**
    - Subtract the initial investment from the total present value of cash inflows.

Example Calculation

Assumptions:

- **Initial Investment (C_o):** $100,000
- **Cash Flows Over 5 Years:**
    - Year 1: $30,000
    - Year 2: $40,000
    - Year 3: $50,000
    - Year 4: $60,000
    - Year 5: $70,000
- **Discount Rate (r):** 10% (0.10)
-

Present Value Calculation:

$$PV_{\text{Year 1}} = \frac{30,000}{(1+0.10)^1} = 27,273$$
$$PV_{\text{Year 2}} = \frac{40,000}{(1+0.10)^2} = 33,058$$
$$PV_{\text{Year 3}} = \frac{50,000}{(1+0.10)^3} = 37,688$$
$$PV_{\text{Year 4}} = \frac{60,000}{(1+0.10)^4} = 41,316$$
$$PV_{\text{Year 5}} = \frac{70,000}{(1+0.10)^5} = 43,555$$

Total Present Value of Cash Flows:

Total PV=27,273+33,058+37,688+41,316+43,555=182,890

Calculate NPV:

NPV=182,890−100,000=82,890

Interpretation

- If NPV > 0: The project is expected to generate value and is considered a good investment.
- If NPV = 0: The project breaks even, generating just enough returns to cover costs.
- If NPV < 0: The project is expected to result in a loss and may be rejected.

Pros and Cons of NPV

Pros:

- **Time Value of Money:** Considers the time value of money, providing a more accurate reflection of investment value.
- **Comprehensive Evaluation:** Accounts for all cash flows over the project's lifespan, giving a complete picture of profitability.
- **Decision-Making Tool:** A clear indicator for guiding investment decisions.

Cons:

- **Complexity:** Requires accurate estimates of future cash flows, which can be difficult to predict.
- **Sensitive to Assumptions:** The outcome is sensitive to the chosen discount rate and cash flow projections.
- **Less Useful for Short-Term Projects:** More beneficial for long-term investments, where cash flows are more variable.

Applications in Software Project Management

1. **Project Selection:** Use NPV to evaluate and prioritize software projects based on expected profitability.
2. **Budgeting and Forecasting:** Incorporate NPV in budgeting processes to assess the financial viability of software initiatives.
3. **Performance Monitoring:** Track NPV over time to evaluate ongoing project performance against initial expectations.

2.5.5 Internal Rate of Return (IRR)

The Internal Rate of Return (IRR) is the discount rate that makes the Net Present Value (NPV) of a project equal to zero. It represents the expected annualized rate of return on an investment, helping decision-makers evaluate the profitability of a project.

Formula: The IRR is calculated using the NPV formula set to zero:

$$0 - \sum \left(\frac{C_t}{(1 + \text{IRR})^t} \right) - C_0$$

Where:

- C_t = Cash inflow during the period ttt
- C_0 = Initial investment
- t= Time period

Importance of IRR in Software Project Management

1. **Investment Decision-Making:** IRR helps in deciding whether to undertake a project by comparing it to a required rate of return or cost of capital.

2. **Project Comparison:** Facilitates comparison between multiple projects or investments, aiding in prioritization.
3. **Performance Benchmarking:** Offers a standard for assessing the efficiency of investments over time.

Calculating IRR

1. **Estimate Cash Flows:**
    - Identify all expected cash inflows and outflows associated with the project.
2. **Set NPV to Zero:**
    - Use trial and error, interpolation, or financial software/calculators to find the IRR that sets the NPV equation to zero.

Example Calculation

Assumptions:

- **Initial Investment (C_0):** \$100,000
- **Cash Flows Over 5 Years:**
    - Year 1: \$30,000
    - Year 2: \$40,000
    - Year 3: \$50,000
    - Year 4: \$60,000
    - Year 5: \$70,000

Step-by-Step Calculation

1. **Set Up the Equation:**

$$0 = -100,000 + \frac{30,000}{(1+\text{IRR})^1} + \frac{40,000}{(1+\text{IRR})^2} + \frac{50,000}{(1+\text{IRR})^3} + \frac{60,000}{(1+\text{IRR})^4} + \frac{70,0}{(1+\text{IR}}$$

2. **Use Financial Tools:**

- Most financial calculators or spreadsheet software (e.g., Excel) can compute IRR using built-in functions.

In Excel, you can use the =IRR () function:

```excel
=IRR([-100000, 30000, 40000, 50000, 60000, 70000])
```

Interpretation

- If **IRR > required rate of return:** The project is likely a good investment.
- If **IRR = required rate of return:** The project breaks even.
- If **IRR < required rate of return:** The project may not be worth pursuing.

Pros and Cons of IRR

Pros:

- **Time Value of Money:** Takes into account the time value of money, providing a realistic measure of profitability.
- **Easy to Understand:** Provides a single percentage that represents the return on investment, making it easy for stakeholders to grasp.
- **Comparison Across Projects:** Facilitates comparison of projects with different scales and durations.

Cons:

- **Multiple IRRs:** Projects with non-conventional cash flows may yield multiple IRRs, complicating decision-making.
- **Overestimation Risk:** IRR can overstate the potential returns when used for mutually exclusive projects.
- **Assumes Reinvestment Rate:** Assumes that cash inflows are reinvested at the same rate as the IRR, which may not be realistic.

Applications in Software Project Management

1. **Project Selection:** Use IRR to evaluate and prioritize software projects based on expected returns.
2. **Budgeting:** Incorporate IRR into budgeting discussions to align projects with strategic financial goals.
3. **Performance Monitoring:** Track IRR over time to assess ongoing project performance and adjust strategies accordingly.

2.6 Risk Evaluation

Risk evaluation is the process of identifying, analyzing, and prioritizing risks associated with a software project. It helps teams understand potential issues that could impact project success and informs strategies for managing these risks.

Importance of Risk Evaluation

1. **Proactive Management:** Identifying risks early allows for proactive measures to mitigate their impact.
2. **Informed Decision-Making:** Provides stakeholders with a clear understanding of potential challenges and uncertainties.
3. **Resource Allocation:** Helps allocate resources effectively to manage high-priority risks.
4. **Increased Success Rates:** Projects with thorough risk evaluation tend to have higher success rates and fewer unforeseen challenges.

Steps in Risk Evaluation

1. **Identify Risks:**
    - **Techniques:** Brainstorming sessions, interviews, checklists, and expert judgment.
    - **Categories:** Technical risks, project management risks, organizational risks, external risks (e.g., regulatory changes).
2. **Analyze Risks:**
    - **Qualitative Analysis:** Assess the impact and likelihood of each risk on a scale (e.g., high, medium, low).
    - **Quantitative Analysis:** Assign numerical values to risks (e.g., potential financial impact) using statistical methods.
3. **Prioritize Risks:**
    - Create a risk matrix to prioritize risks based on their likelihood and impact. This helps focus on the most significant threats.
4. **Develop Response Strategies:**
    - **Avoid:** Alter project plans to eliminate the risk.
    - **Mitigate:** Implement measures to reduce the impact or likelihood of the risk.
    - **Transfer:** Shift the risk to a third party (e.g., insurance or outsourcing).
    - **Accept:** Acknowledge the risk and decide to proceed, often with contingency plans.
5. **Monitor and Review:**
    - Continuously track identified risks and monitor for new risks throughout the project lifecycle. Regularly review and update risk management strategies.

Risk Evaluation Techniques

1. **Risk Register:**
   - A document that records identified risks, their analysis, response strategies, and status. It serves as a living document throughout the project.
2. **SWOT Analysis:**
   - Assess strengths, weaknesses, opportunities, and threats to identify internal and external risks.
3. **Failure Mode and Effects Analysis (FMEA):**
   - A systematic approach to evaluate potential failure modes within a system and their causes and effects.
4. **Monte Carlo Simulation:**
   - A quantitative risk analysis technique that uses statistical modeling to predict potential outcomes based on varying risk factors.
5. **Scenario Analysis:**
   - Develop different scenarios to understand how various risks could impact project outcomes.

Risk Evaluation Metrics

1. **Risk Exposure:**
   - Calculated as the product of the likelihood of a risk occurring and its impact.

   $$\text{Risk Exposure} = \text{Likelihood} \times \text{Impact}$$

2. **Risk Mitigation Effectiveness:**
   - Measure the effectiveness of risk responses over time to ensure continuous improvement.

Tools for Risk Evaluation

1. **Risk Management Software:** Tools like Jira, Trello, or dedicated risk management platforms help track risks and facilitate communication among team members.
2. **Spreadsheets:** Simple tools like Excel can be used to create risk registers and analyze risks.
3. **Gantt Charts:** Visual representation of project timelines that help identify dependencies and potential risk areas.

Best Practices

1. **Engage Stakeholders:**
    - Involve team members, stakeholders, and experts in the risk evaluation process to gain diverse perspectives.
2. **Regular Updates:**
    - Continuously update the risk register and evaluation strategies as the project progresses and new information emerges.
3. **Communicate Risks:**
    - Ensure that risks and their management strategies are communicated clearly to all stakeholders.
4. **Establish a Risk Culture:**
    - Foster an organizational culture that values risk awareness and proactive management.

2.6.1 Identification and Ranking

This process helps teams prioritize risks and develop effective mitigation strategies.

Steps in Risk Identification

1. Identify Risks

- **Brainstorming Sessions:** Engage team members and stakeholders to discuss potential risks.
- **Checklists:** Use predefined lists of common risks in software projects (e.g., technical challenges, scope creep).
- **Interviews:** Conduct interviews with experienced stakeholders or experts to gather insights.
- **Historical Data Analysis:** Review past projects for lessons learned and risk occurrences.

2. Categorize Risks

- **Technical Risks:** Issues related to technology, architecture, or performance.
- **Project Management Risks:** Schedule delays, resource allocation, or scope changes.
- **Organizational Risks:** Changes in management, team dynamics, or organizational policies.
- **External Risks:** Market changes, regulatory issues, or vendor dependencies.

Risk Ranking Process

3. **Analyze Risks**

- **Qualitative Analysis:** Assess risks based on their likelihood and impact using a scale (e.g., high, medium, low).
- **Quantitative Analysis:** Assign numerical values to risks, if applicable, to facilitate further analysis.

4. **Create a Risk Matrix**

- A risk matrix helps visualize and prioritize risks by plotting them on a grid based on their likelihood and impact.

Likelihood/Impact	**Low (1)**	**Medium (2)**	**High (3)**
High (3)	Medium	High	Critical
Medium (2)	Low	Medium	High
Low (1)	Low	Low	Medium

5. **Rank Risks**

- Calculate a **Risk Score** using the formula:

$$\text{Risk Score} = \text{Likelihood} \times \text{Impact}$$

- This score helps prioritize risks for action.

Risk Ranking Example

Assumptions:

- **Likelihood Scale (1-3):** 1 (Low), 2 (Medium), 3 (High)
- **Impact Scale (1-3):** 1 (Low), 2 (Medium), 3 (High)

Risk	**Likelihood**	**Impact**	**Risk Score**
Inadequate requirements	3	3	9
Team turnover	2	3	6
Technical debt	3	2	6
Scope creep	2	3	6
Regulatory changes	1	2	2

Risk Ranking:

- **Critical:** Inadequate requirements (Score: 9)
- **High:** Team turnover, Technical debt, Scope creep (Score: 6)
- **Low:** Regulatory changes (Score: 2)

Risk Response Strategies

6. **Develop Mitigation Plans**

- **Avoid:** Change project plans to eliminate the risk.
- **Mitigate:** Implement actions to reduce the likelihood or impact of the risk.
- **Transfer:** Shift the risk to a third party (e.g., insurance).
- **Accept:** Acknowledge the risk and plan to monitor it without action.

2.6.2 Cost Benefit Analysis

Cost-benefit analysis (CBA) is a critical evaluation technique in software project management that helps assess the financial implications of risks. It compares the costs of implementing risk mitigation strategies against the expected benefits, providing a clear picture of whether a particular action is worthwhile.

Importance of Cost-Benefit Analysis

1. Informed Decision-Making: Helps project managers make data-driven decisions regarding risk management strategies.
2. Resource Allocation: Ensures that resources are allocated efficiently by highlighting the most beneficial risk responses.
3. Stakeholder Communication: Provides a clear rationale for risk management choices, facilitating communication with stakeholders.

Steps in Conducting Cost-Benefit Analysis

1. **Identify Risks and Mitigation Strategies**

- List identified risks and potential mitigation strategies.
- Example risks: technical debt, team turnover, security vulnerabilities.

2. **Estimate Costs of Mitigation**

- Calculate the costs associated with each risk mitigation strategy, including:
  - Direct costs (e.g., hiring additional staff, purchasing tools)
  - Indirect costs (e.g., training, potential delays)

Example:

- **Technical Debt Mitigation:** $20,000 for refactoring code.

3. **Estimate Benefits of Mitigation**

- Determine the expected benefits from mitigating the risk, such as:
  - Reduced likelihood of failure
  - Cost savings from avoiding issues
  - Increased project efficiency or customer satisfaction

Example:

- **Technical Debt Mitigation:** Expected savings of $50,000 from reduced bugs and maintenance.

4. **Calculate Net Benefits**

- Use the formula:

$$\text{Net Benefits} = \text{Total Benefits} - \text{Total Costs}$$

Example:

- **Net Benefits for Technical Debt:** $50,000 (benefits) - $20,000 (costs) = $30,000

5. **Perform Sensitivity Analysis**

- Assess how changes in assumptions (e.g., costs or benefits) impact the analysis. This helps understand the robustness of the decision.

6. **Make Informed Decisions**

- Compare the net benefits of different mitigation strategies and prioritize actions based on their CBA outcomes.

Example of Cost-Benefit Analysis

Scenario

Risk: Inadequate Requirements

1. **Mitigation Strategy:** Implement additional stakeholder engagement sessions.

2. **Cost Estimation:**
    - Additional workshops: $15,000
    - Extra documentation: $5,000
    - **Total Costs:** $20,000
3. **Benefit Estimation:**
    - Reduced rework and delays: $50,000
    - Improved project alignment: $30,000
    - **Total Benefits:** $80,000
4. **Net Benefits Calculation:**

    Net Benefits=80,000−20,000=60,000

Summary Table

Risk	**Mitigation Strategy**	**Costs**	**Benefits**	**Net Benefits**
Inadequate Requirements	Stakeholder engagement sessions	$20,000	$80,000	$60,000
Technical Debt	Code refactoring	$20,000	$50,000	$30,000
Team Turnover	Employee training and retention	$15,000	$40,000	$25,000

2.6.3 Risk Profile Analysis

Risk Profile Analysis is a systematic approach used in software project management to identify, assess, and prioritize risks. This method helps teams understand the overall risk landscape of a project and make informed decisions regarding risk management strategies.

Importance of Risk Profile Analysis

1. **Holistic View:** Provides a comprehensive overview of all potential risks in a project, enabling better understanding and management.
2. **Prioritization:** Helps prioritize risks based on their impact and likelihood, ensuring that critical risks receive attention.
3. **Informed Decision-Making:** Facilitates strategic planning and decision-making by highlighting areas that require mitigation efforts.
4. **Stakeholder Communication:** A clear representation of risks helps communicate potential challenges to stakeholders effectively.

Steps in Conducting Risk Profile Analysis

1. **Identify Risks**

- Use techniques such as brainstorming, checklists, interviews, and historical data analysis to identify potential risks associated with the project.

2. **Assess Risks**

- Evaluate each identified risk based on two primary dimensions:
  - **Likelihood:** The probability that a risk will occur.
  - **Impact:** The potential consequences or severity of the risk if it occurs.

3. **Create a Risk Matrix**

- Develop a risk matrix to visualize the likelihood and impact of each risk. This helps categorize risks into different levels.

Likelihood / Impact	**Low (1)**	**Medium (2)**	**High (3)**
High (3)	Medium	High	Critical
Medium (2)	Low	Medium	High
Low (1)	Low	Low	Medium

4. **Rank Risks**

- Assign risk scores using the formula:

$$\text{Risk Score} = \text{Likelihood} \times \text{Impact}$$

- Use these scores to prioritize risks for further action.

5. **Develop Risk Profiles**

- Create a risk profile for the project, summarizing the most significant risks based on their scores and categories.

6. **Monitor and Review**

- Continuously monitor the identified risks and update the risk profile as the project progresses. This ensures that new risks are identified and existing risks are reassessed.

Example of Risk Profile Analysis

Scenario: Software Development Project

Identified Risks

Risk	Likelihood (1-3)	Impact (1-3)	Risk Score
Inadequate requirements	3	3	9
Technical debt	2	3	6
Team turnover	2	2	4
Scope creep	3	2	6
Regulatory changes	1	2	2

Risk Matrix Visualization

Risk	Impact Level	Risk Level
Inadequate requirements	High (3)	Critical (9)
Technical debt	High (3)	High (6)
Team turnover	Medium (2)	High (6)
Scope creep	Medium (2)	Medium (4)
Regulatory changes	Low (1)	Low (2)

Summary of Risk Profile

Risk	Risk Score	Risk Level	Response Strategy
Inadequate requirements	9	Critical	Engage stakeholders
Technical debt	6	High	Refactor code
Team turnover	6	High	Strict scope management
Scope creep	4	Medium	Training and retention
Regulatory changes	2	Low	Monitor regulations

2.6.4 Using Decision Trees

Decision trees are a valuable tool for risk evaluation in software project management. They provide a visual representation of decisions, potential risks, and their consequences, helping project managers make informed choices.

Importance of Decision Trees

Visual Clarity: Decision trees offer a clear graphical representation of decisions and their potential outcomes, making complex risk scenarios easier to understand.

Structured Analysis: They facilitate structured analysis by breaking down decisions into smaller, manageable parts.

Quantitative Assessment: Decision trees allow for the incorporation of probabilities and financial impacts, aiding in quantitative risk assessment.

Steps to Create a Decision Tree

1. Define the Decision Problem

Clearly outline the decision to be made, including the specific risks involved.

2. Identify Possible Alternatives

List all possible actions or strategies that can be taken in response to the identified risks.

3. Determine Outcomes and Probabilities

For each alternative, identify potential outcomes and assign probabilities based on historical data or expert judgment.

4. Assign Values to Outcomes

Estimate the financial impact or utility of each outcome, which will help in calculating expected values.

5. Construct the Decision Tree

Create the tree by branching out from the initial decision point to the possible alternatives, outcomes, and associated probabilities and values.

6. Analyze the Decision Tree

Calculate the expected values for each decision path and compare them to identify the most favorable option.

Example of Using a Decision Tree

Scenario: Choosing Between Two Software Development Approaches

Step 1: Define the Decision Problem

You must decide between two approaches for a software project: In-House Development vs. Outsourcing.

Step 2: Identify Possible Alternatives

In-House Development

Outsourcing

Step 3: Determine Outcomes and Probabilities

Approach	**Outcome**	**Probability**	**Value ($)**
In-House Development	Successful	0.6	200,000
In-House Development	Unsuccessful	0.4	-50,000
Outsourcing	Successful	0.8	150,000
Outsourcing	**Unsuccessful**	**0.2**	**-30,000**

Step 4: Assign Values to Outcomes

Successful projects lead to profit, while unsuccessful ones lead to losses.

Step 5: Construct the Decision Tree

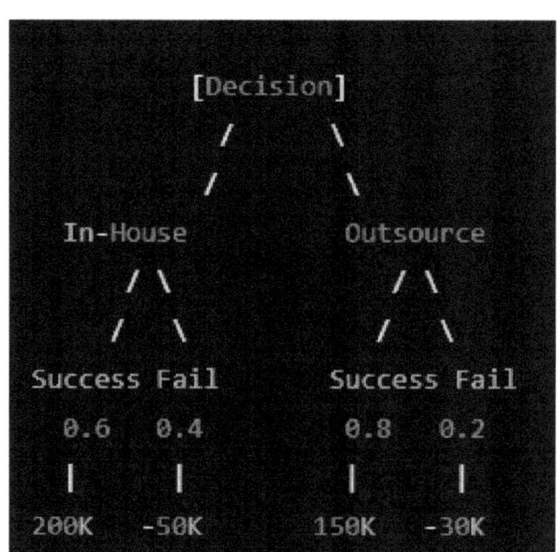

Step 6: Analyze the Decision Tree

Calculate Expected Values:

- **In-House Development:**

$$EV=(0.6\times200{,}000)+(0.4\times-50{,}000)=120{,}000-20{,}000=100{,}000$$

- **Outsourcing:**

$$EV=(0.8\times150{,}000)+(0.2\times-30{,}000)=120{,}000-6{,}000=114{,}000$$

Conclusion from Analysis

In-House Development EV: $100,000

Outsourcing EV: $114,000

Given the expected values, outsourcing is the more favorable option.

Advantages of Using Decision Trees

Clarity: Provides a straightforward way to visualize complex decisions and their consequences.

Risk Quantification: Allows for the integration of probabilities and financial impacts, enabling a quantitative assessment of risks.

Facilitates Communication: Aids in explaining decisions to stakeholders through a clear visual format.

Disadvantages of Using Decision Trees

Complexity with Many Variables: Decision trees can become complex and unwieldy with numerous variables and outcomes.

Estimation Challenges: Assigning probabilities and values can be subjective and may lead to inaccuracies if not based on solid data.

Chapter 3

ACTIVITY PLANNING

Activity planning is a critical component of software project management that involves identifying, organizing, and scheduling project activities to ensure successful project delivery. This process helps in defining the scope of work, allocating resources, and managing timelines effectively.

Importance of Activity Planning

1. **Clear Direction:** Provides a roadmap for project execution, ensuring all team members understand their roles and responsibilities.
2. **Resource Allocation:** Facilitates effective allocation of resources, including time, personnel, and budget.
3. **Risk Management:** Identifies potential risks associated with activities and allows for proactive mitigation strategies.
4. **Performance Monitoring:** Establishes benchmarks for measuring progress and performance throughout the project lifecycle.

Steps in Activity Planning

1. **Define Project Scope**
   - Outline the project objectives, deliverables, and boundaries to establish what will and will not be included.
2. **Identify Activities**
   - Break down the project into smaller, manageable activities or tasks. Use techniques like:
     - **Work Breakdown Structure (WBS):** Decomposes the project into hierarchical levels of work.
     - **Brainstorming:** Gather input from team members to identify all necessary activities.
3. **Sequence Activities**
   - Determine the order in which activities need to be performed. Consider dependencies (e.g., which tasks must be completed before others can start).
   - Techniques include:
     - **Precedence Diagramming Method (PDM)**
     - **Dependency Relationships (Finish-to-Start, Start-to-Start, etc.)**
4. **Estimate Duration**
   - Estimate the time required to complete each activity. Use historical data, expert judgment, or estimation techniques like:
     - **Three-point estimation (Optimistic, Pessimistic, Most Likely)**

5. **Assign Resources**
   - Identify and allocate the necessary resources for each activity, including team members, tools, and budget.
6. **Develop a Schedule**
   - Create a project schedule using tools like Gantt charts or project management software this visual representation helps track progress and manages timelines.
7. **Monitor and Adjust**
   - Continuously monitor the progress of activities, making adjustments as necessary to stay on track and address any emerging issues.

Tools for Activity Planning

1. **Gantt Charts:** Visual representation of the project schedule, showing activity durations and dependencies.
2. **Project Management Software:** Tools like Microsoft Project, Trello, or Asana for managing tasks and timelines.
3. **Work Breakdown Structure (WBS):** Helps organize tasks and visualize project components.
4. **Critical Path Method (CPM):** Identifies the longest sequence of dependent tasks to determine the minimum project duration.

Example of Activity Planning

Project: Developing a New Software Application

Step 1: Define Project Scope

Objective: Develop a web application for customer relationship management (CRM).

Deliverables: Functional software, user documentation, training materials.

Step 2: Identify Activities (using WBS)

I. Requirements Gathering
   Stakeholder Interviews
   Document Requirements

II. Design
   Create UI/UX Designs
   Develop System Architecture
   Development

III. Frontend Development
   Backend Development

IV. Testing
   Unit Testing
   User Acceptance Testing (UAT)

V. Deployment
   Deploy to Production
   Conduct Training Sessions

Step 3: Sequence Activities
Example dependencies:
Requirements Gathering must be completed before Design starts.
Design must be completed before Development can commence.
Step 4: Estimate Duration

Activity	Estimated Duration
Stakeholder Interviews	1 week
Document Requirements	2 weeks
Create UI/UX Designs	2 weeks
Frontend Development	4 weeks
Backend Development	4 weeks
Unit Testing	2 weeks
User Acceptance Testing (UAT)	1 week
Deploy to Production	1 week
Conduct Training Sessions	1 week

Step 5: Assign Resources
Assign team members to each activity based on skills and availability.
Step 6: Develop a Schedule
Create a Gantt chart to visualize the project timeline, showing start and end dates for each activity.
Step 7: Monitor and Adjust
Regularly review progress against the schedule, making adjustments as needed to address delays or resource constraints.

3.1 Project Schedule / Activity Schedule

An activity schedule is a vital part of project scheduling in software project management. It outlines the timeline for project activities, ensuring that tasks are completed on time and within scope. A well-structured activity schedule is essential for successful project execution and monitoring.
Importance of Activity Schedule

1. **Time Management:** Helps allocate time effectively to each activity, ensuring timely project completion.
2. **Resource Allocation:** Assists in planning resource usage throughout the project, preventing over allocation or conflicts.
3. **Progress Tracking:** Provides a framework for monitoring project progress against deadlines.

4. **Stakeholder Communication:** Facilitates communication with stakeholders regarding project timelines and milestones.

Steps to Create an Activity Schedule

1. **Define Project Scope and Activities**
    - Clearly outline the project objectives and deliverables.
    - Break down the project into smaller, manageable activities using a **Work Breakdown Structure (WBS)**.

2. **Estimate Activity Durations**
    - Estimate the time required for each activity. Techniques include:
        - **Expert judgment**
        - **Historical data**
        - **Three-point estimation (Optimistic, Pessimistic, Most Likely)**
3. **Sequence Activities**
    - Determine the order of activities based on dependencies. Use techniques such as:
        - **Precedence Diagramming Method (PDM)**
        - Identify dependency types (Finish-to-Start, Start-to-Start, etc.).
4. **Assign Resources**
    - Identify and allocate resources (team members, tools, etc.) for each activity.
5. **Develop the Schedule**
    - Create the activity schedule using tools like Gantt charts or project management software. Include:
        - Start and end dates
        - Milestones
        - Dependencies
6. **Monitor and Update the Schedule**
    - Continuously track progress against the activity schedule, updating it as necessary to reflect changes or delays.

Example of an Activity Schedule

Project: Developing a Customer Relationship Management (CRM) System

Step 1: Define Activities

Activity	Description
Requirements Gathering	Collect and document requirements
Design	Create UI/UX and system architecture
Development	Build frontend and backend components
Testing	Conduct unit and user acceptance testing
Deployment	Deploy the application to production
Training	Conduct user training sessions

Step 2: Estimate Durations

Activity	Estimated Duration
Requirements Gathering	2 weeks
Design	3 weeks
Development	6 weeks
Testing	2 weeks
Deployment	1 week
Training	1 week

Step 3: Sequence Activities

Activity	Predecessors
Requirements Gathering	-
Design	Requirements Gathering
Development	Design
Testing	Development
Deployment	Testing
Training	Deployment

Step 4: Assign Resources

Activity	Assigned Resources
Requirements Gathering	Business Analyst
Design	UI/UX Designer
Development	Developers
Testing	QA Team
Deployment	DevOps Engineer
Training	Project Manager

Step 5: Develop the Schedule

Activity	Start Date	End Date
Requirements Gathering	Week 1	Week 2
Design	Week 3	Week 5
Development	Week 6	Week 11
Testing	Week 12	Week 13
Deployment	Week 14	Week 14
Training	Week 15	Week 15

Gantt chart Representation

A Gantt chart visually represents the above schedule, showing timelines for each activity and their dependencies.

```lua
| Activity               | Week 1 | Week 2 | Week 3 | Week 4 | Week 5 | Week 6 | Week 7 |
|------------------------|--------|--------|--------|--------|--------|--------|--------|-
| Requirements Gathering | ████████ |      |        |        |        |        |        |
| Design                 |        |        | ██████████ | ████████ |    |        |        |
| Development            |        |        |        |        |        | ██████████████
| Testing                |        |        |        |        |        |        |        |
| Deployment             |        |        |        |        |        |        |        |
| Training               |        |        |        |        |        |        |        |
```

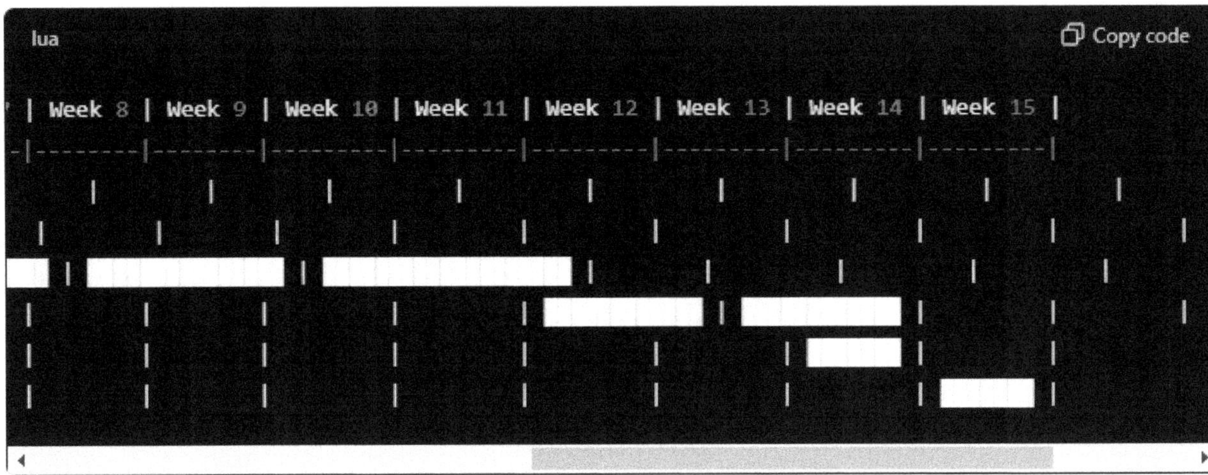

Step 6: Monitor and Update the Schedule

Regularly check the progress of each activity against the schedule and make necessary adjustments to address any delays or issues that arise.

3.2 Sequencing and Scheduling Activities

Sequencing Activities

1. **Identify Activities**:
   - List all tasks required to complete the project.
2. **Define Dependencies**:
   - Determine relationships between tasks (e.g., finish-to-start, start-to-start).
3. **Create a Network Diagram**:
   - Visualize tasks and their dependencies using flowcharts or diagrams.
4. **Prioritize Tasks**:
   - Rank tasks based on importance and dependencies to identify critical paths.

Scheduling Activities

1. **Estimate Duration**:
   - Assess the time required to complete each task using historical data or expert judgment.
2. **Develop a Schedule**:
   - Use tools like Gantt charts or project management software to outline the timeline for tasks.
3. **Assign Resources**:
   - Allocate team members and tools to tasks based on availability and skillsets.
4. **Establish Milestones**:
   - Identify key milestones to mark significant points in the project timeline.
5. **Monitor and Adjust**:
   - Regularly review progress against the schedule and adjust timelines or resources as necessary.

Tools and Techniques

- **Gantt Charts**: Visual representation of the schedule, showing start and finish dates.
- **Critical Path Method (CPM)**: Identifies the longest sequence of dependent tasks and helps in prioritizing scheduling.
- **PERT Charts**: Used for estimating project duration by analyzing task time variability.

Best Practices

- **Regular Updates**: Keep the schedule updated based on project progress and changes.
- **Communication**: Ensure team members are aware of their responsibilities and deadlines.
- **Flexibility**: Be prepared to adapt the schedule in response to unforeseen challenges.

By effectively sequencing and scheduling activities, you can enhance project organization and improve the likelihood of timely delivery.

3.3 Network Planning Models

1. Critical Path Method (CPM)

- **Purpose**: Identifies the longest path of dependent tasks and determines the shortest possible project duration.
- **Key Components**:
    - **Nodes**: Represent tasks or milestones.
    - **Edges**: Represent dependencies between tasks.
- **Benefits**:
    - Highlights critical tasks that cannot be delayed without affecting the project timeline.
    - Helps in resource allocation and prioritization.

2. Program Evaluation and Review Technique (PERT)

- **Purpose**: Analyzes the time required to complete each task and estimates project duration with uncertainty.
- **Key Components**:
    - Uses three time estimates for each task: optimistic, pessimistic, and most likely.
- **Benefits**:
    - Provides a probability distribution of project completion time.
    - Useful for projects with high uncertainty in task durations.

3. Precedence Diagramming Method (PDM)

- **Purpose**: Visualizes task sequences and dependencies in a network format.
- **Key Components**:
    - Tasks are represented by boxes (nodes), and arrows indicate relationships.
- **Types of Dependencies**:
    - Finish-to-Start (FS)
    - Start-to-Start (SS)
    - Finish-to-Finish (FF)
    - Start-to-Finish (SF)

- **Benefits**:
  - Clear representation of task relationships and timelines.

4. Gantt Charts

- **Purpose**: Provides a visual representation of the project schedule over time.
- **Key Components**:
  - Horizontal bars represent task durations along a timeline.
- **Benefits**:
  - Easy to understand and communicate project status.
  - Helps in tracking progress against the schedule.

5. Resource-Oriented Network Planning

- **Purpose**: Focuses on resource allocation and constraints within the project network.
- **Key Components**:
  - Tasks are prioritized based on resource availability and workload balancing.
- **Benefits**:
  - Ensures optimal use of resources while maintaining project timelines.

Implementation Steps

1. **Define Activities**: Identify all tasks required for the project.
2. **Determine Dependencies**: Establish relationships between tasks.
3. **Develop Network Diagram**: Create a visual representation of the tasks and their dependencies.
4. **Analyze the Network**: Use CPM or PERT to find critical paths and estimate project duration.
5. **Update Regularly**: Continuously monitor and adjust the network model as the project progresses.

3.4 Forward Pass and Backward Pass

Forward Pass

Purpose: To determine the earliest start and finish times for each activity in a project.

Steps:

1. **Start with the First Activity**:
   - Set the earliest start (ES) time of the first activity to 0.
2. **Calculate Early Start and Finish**:
   - For each subsequent activity:
     - **Early Start (ES)**: The earliest time an activity can start. It is determined by the finish time of predecessor activities.
     - **Early Finish (EF)**: Calculated as: EF=ES+Duration
3. **Continue through the Network**:
   - Move through the network diagram from the start to the end, calculating ES and EF for each task.

Example:

- **Activity A**: Duration = 5 days, ES = 0, EF = 5
- **Activity B (depends on A)**: Duration = 3 days, ES = 5, EF = 8

Backward Pass

Purpose: To determine the latest start and finish times for each activity, helping to identify slack time.

Steps:

1. **Start with the Last Activity**:
   - Set the latest finish (LF) time of the last activity to its early finish time.
2. **Calculate Late Finish and Start**:
   - For each preceding activity:
     - **Late Finish (LF)**: The latest time an activity can finish without delaying the project. For the last activity, this is equal to EF.
     - **Late Start (LS)**: Calculated as: LS=LF−Duration\text{LS} = \text{LF} - \text{Duration}LS=LF−Duration
3. **Continue through the Network**:
   - Move backward through the network diagram to calculate LF and LS for each task.

Example:

- **Activity B**: Duration = 3 days, LF = 8, LS = 5
- **Activity A (depends on B)**: LF = 5, LS = 0

Slack Time

- **Slack (or Float)**: The amount of time an activity can be delayed without affecting the overall project duration. Calculated as: Slack=LS−ES or Slack=LF−EF

Importance

- **Forward Pass**: Helps in understanding the project timeline and critical path.
- **Backward Pass**: Identifies flexibility in scheduling and highlights potential bottlenecks

3.5 Activity Float

In software project management, an "activity float" refers to the amount of time that a particular activity can be delayed without delaying the entire project. It is also known as "float time" or "slack."

Understanding Activity Float:

1. **Definition**: Activity float is the difference between the earliest and latest possible start (or finish) times of an activity without affecting the project schedule.
2. **Calculation**: It is computed during the Critical Path Method (CPM) or Program Evaluation and Review Technique (PERT) analysis. Activities on the critical path have zero float, meaning any delay in these activities directly impacts the project timeline.
3. **Types**:

- **Total Float**: The total amount of time an activity can be delayed without delaying the project completion.
- **Free Float**: The amount of time an activity can be delayed without delaying the early start of any successor activity.
- **Project Float**: The amount of time the entire project can be delayed without delaying external deadlines or commitments.

4. **Importance**:
   - Helps project managers identify activities that have flexibility in their schedules.
   - Allows for better resource allocation and scheduling adjustments.
   - Provides a buffer against unexpected delays or changes.
5. **Management**:
   - Project managers monitor float to ensure activities are completed within their float time to maintain project deadlines.
   - Float can be used strategically to optimize resources or adjust project schedules.

Example:
Imagine a software development project where Activity A, B, and C are sequential with dependencies. Activity A has a total float of 5 days, Activity B has 0 days, and Activity C has 3 days. This means:

- Activity A can be delayed by up to 5 days without affecting subsequent activities or the project completion.
- Activity B must start on time as it is on the critical path.
- Activity C can be delayed by up to 3 days without delaying the project.

Understanding and managing activity float is crucial for effective project planning and execution in software development, helping teams deliver projects on time and within budget.

3.6 Shortening Project Duration

Shortening project duration in software project management involves various strategies and considerations to compress the timeline without compromising quality or increasing risks excessively. Here are some effective approaches:

1. Critical Path Analysis:

- **Identify critical activities:** Focus on activities that are on the critical path, as these determine the shortest possible project duration.
- **Optimize critical path:** Look for opportunities to streamline critical activities, reduce their durations, or overlap sequential activities if possible (fast-tracking).

2. Resource Allocation:

- **Allocate additional resources:** Assign more resources (human, technological) to critical activities to expedite their completion.
- **Resource leveling:** Balance resource utilization across non-critical activities to avoid delays caused by resource constraints.

3. Scope Management:

- **Scope prioritization:** Focus on delivering essential features first (minimum viable product) and defer non-essential features to later phases or releases.
- **Scope reduction:** If feasible, reduce the scope of the project by eliminating less critical features or functionalities.

4. Risk Management:

- **Identify and mitigate risks:** Address potential risks proactively to prevent delays and disruptions.
- **Contingency planning:** Have contingency plans in place for identified risks to minimize their impact on project schedule.

5. Parallelization and Overlap:

- **Fast-tracking:** Sequential activities that do not depend on each other can be overlapped to shorten the overall duration.
- **Concurrent development:** If feasible, allow teams to work on different parts of the project simultaneously to save time.

6. Efficiency and Process Improvement:

- **Streamline processes:** Identify and eliminate bottlenecks or inefficiencies in workflows and processes.
- **Automate tasks:** Utilize automation tools and techniques to reduce manual effort and accelerate repetitive tasks.

7. Communication and Collaboration:

- **Enhance communication:** Ensure clear and effective communication among team members, stakeholders, and clients to minimize misunderstandings and delays.
- **Collaborative decision-making:** Involve relevant stakeholders in decision-making processes to expedite approvals and reduce decision turnaround times.

8. Monitoring and Adjustments:

- **Regular monitoring:** Continuously monitor project progress against the revised schedule to identify any deviations early.
- **Iterative adjustments:** Make iterative adjustments to the project plan as necessary based on real-time data and feedback.

Example Scenario:

Imagine a software project originally planned for 6 months. By implementing the strategies above, the project manager identifies critical activities, assigns additional resources to speed up development, and fast-tracks certain tasks. Scope is prioritized to focus on core functionalities first, with less critical features deferred to a later phase. Regular communication ensures everyone is aligned, and risks are managed proactively.

By carefully applying these strategies, the project manager successfully shortens the project duration to 4 months while maintaining quality and minimizing risks, meeting client expectations and business deadlines effectively.

3.7 Activity on Arrow Network

In software project management, the Activity on Arrow (AOA) network, also known as the Arrow Diagramming Method (ADM), is a graphical representation technique used for scheduling and planning activities within a project. Here's how it works and its key components:

Components of Activity on Arrow (AOA) Network:

1. **Nodes (Events):**
    - Represent significant points in time during a project's lifecycle.
    - Usually depicted as circles or nodes.
    - Events are points where activities start, finish, or intersect.
2. **Arrows (Activities):**
    - Represent activities or tasks that must be completed.
    - Directed arrows connect nodes and indicate the sequence of activities.
    - Arrows have labels that denote the activity identifier and duration.
3. **Dummy Activities:**
    - Used to represent logical relationships between events that don't involve actual work but are necessary for sequencing.
    - Denoted by dashed lines with no duration or resources assigned.

Advantages of AOA Network:

- **Visualization:** Provides a clear visual representation of task dependencies and sequencing.
- **Logical Relationships:** Shows logical relationships between activities, such as start-to-start, finish-to-start, etc.
- **Critical Path Analysis:** Facilitates identification of the critical path and non-critical paths within the project.
- **Efficiency:** Helps in optimizing resource allocation and scheduling by clearly outlining dependencies.

Steps to Develop an AOA Network:

1. **Identify Activities:**
    - List all activities or tasks required to complete the project.
    - Determine the sequence in which activities must be performed.
2. **Determine Dependencies:**
    - Define the logical relationships (predecessors and successors) between activities.
    - Specify whether activities can start concurrently or if they must be sequenced.
3. **Draw the Network:**
    - Place nodes (events) for project milestones, start, and finish.
    - Draw arrows (activities) between nodes to represent task dependencies.
    - Label arrows with activity identifiers and durations.
4. **Analyze the Network:**
    - Perform critical path analysis to identify the longest path of activities.

    - Determine total project duration and any slack (float) available for non-critical activities.
5. **Update and Monitor:**
    - Regularly update the AOA network as project progresses.
    - Monitor changes in activity durations or dependencies and adjust the network accordingly.

Example:

Consider a software development project with the following activities:

- A: Requirements gathering (5 days)
- B: Design (10 days)
- C: Coding (15 days)
- D: Testing (8 days)
- E: Deployment (3 days)

Logical dependencies:

- A must finish before B can start.
- B must finish before C can start.
- C must finish before D can start.
- D must finish before E can start.

Using AOA network:

- Node 1 (start)
- Node 2 (A finish)
- Node 3 (B finish)
- Node 4 (C finish)
- Node 5 (D finish)
- Node 6 (E finish)

Arrows:

- A: from Node 1 to Node 2 (duration 5 days)
- B: from Node 2 to Node 3 (duration 10 days)
- C: from Node 3 to Node 4 (duration 15 days)
- D: from Node 4 to Node 5 (duration 8 days)
- E: from Node 5 to Node 6 (duration 3 days)

Dummy activities may be used to denote sequencing constraints or logical relationships not directly tied to actual work durations.

In summary, the Activity on Arrow (AOA) network is a valuable tool in software project management for visually representing and planning project activities, dependencies, and critical paths, facilitating efficient scheduling and resource management.

3.8 Risk Management

Risk management in software project management is crucial for identifying, assessing, and mitigating potential risks that could impact project timelines, budgets, and overall success. Here's how risk management is typically approached in activity planning:

1. Risk Identification:

- **Brainstorming sessions:** Engage project stakeholders, team members, and subject matter experts to identify potential risks.
- **Checklists and templates:** Utilize historical data, checklists, and risk templates to systematically identify common risks in software projects (e.g., requirements changes, technology risks, resource constraints).

2. Risk Assessment:

- **Probability and impact analysis:** Assess the likelihood of each identified risk occurring and the potential impact on project objectives (schedule, cost, quality).
- **Risk categorization:** Classify risks into categories (e.g., technical, organizational, external) to prioritize mitigation efforts.

3. Risk Prioritization:

- **Risk ranking:** Prioritize risks based on their combined probability and impact (using risk matrices or qualitative assessments).
- **Focus on high-priority risks:** Allocate resources and attention to risks that pose the greatest threat to project success.

4. Risk Mitigation Strategies:

- **Avoidance:** Modify the project plan to eliminate the risk or adjust activities to reduce exposure.
- **Mitigation:** Implement proactive measures to reduce the probability or impact of risks (e.g., prototype development, early testing).
- **Transfer:** Shift the risk to third parties (e.g., outsourcing, insurance).
- **Acceptance:** Acknowledge the risk without taking specific action, particularly if the cost of mitigation outweighs the potential impact.

5. Risk Monitoring and Control:

- **Regular reviews:** Continuously monitor identified risks throughout the project lifecycle.
- **Trigger points:** Define thresholds or trigger points that indicate when risk response strategies should be activated.
- **Contingency planning:** Develop contingency plans for high-impact risks to minimize disruption if they materialize.

6. Integration with Project Activities:

- **Embedded into project plan:** Integrate risk management activities into the overall project plan and schedule.
- **Iterative process:** Review and update risk assessments and mitigation strategies regularly as project activities progress and new risks emerge.

Example Scenario:

In a software development project, potential risks could include:

- **Technical Risks:** Uncertainty in integrating new technologies.
- **Resource Risks:** Key team members unexpectedly leaving.
- **Schedule Risks:** Delays in third-party dependencies.

Risk management would involve:

- **Identification:** Team discussions and analysis of past projects.
- **Assessment:** Evaluating likelihood and impact.
- **Mitigation:** Allocating resources, adjusting schedules.
- **Monitoring:** Regular reviews and adjustments.

By effectively managing risks, software project managers can enhance project predictability, minimize disruptions, and increase the likelihood of delivering projects on time and within budget.

3.9 Nature of Risk

In software project management, risks can arise from various sources and have diverse impacts on project objectives such as schedule, budget, quality, and scope. Understanding the nature of risks helps project managers proactively identify, assess, and mitigate them. Here are some common types and aspects of risks in software project management:

1. Technical Risks:

- **Technology Complexity:** Challenges associated with integrating new technologies or utilizing complex software frameworks.
- **Performance:** Concerns about meeting performance requirements under varying conditions (e.g., load testing).
- **Compatibility:** Issues arising from compatibility between different software components, platforms, or versions.

2. Requirements and Scope Risks:

- **Changes in Requirements:** Unanticipated changes or additions to project requirements, impacting scope and schedule.
- **Incomplete or Unclear Requirements:** Ambiguities or gaps in requirements documentation leading to misunderstandings or rework.
- **Scope Creep:** Gradual expansion of project scope beyond initial plans, affecting timeline and resources.

3. Schedule Risks:

- **Estimation Errors:** Inaccurate estimation of task durations or dependencies leading to schedule delays.
- **Dependency Risks:** Delays caused by dependencies on external factors or third-party deliverables.
- **Resource Constraints:** Shortages or fluctuations in availability of critical resources (e.g., skilled personnel, equipment).

4. Quality Risks:

- **Defects and Bugs:** Potential for software defects affecting functionality, performance, or security.
- **Testing Risks:** Inadequate testing coverage or insufficient testing environments.
- **Maintainability:** Challenges related to the ease of maintaining and updating the software post-deployment.

5. Organizational Risks:

- **Team Dynamics:** Issues related to team collaboration, communication, or conflicts impacting productivity.
- **Stakeholder Expectations:** Misalignment between stakeholder expectations and project deliverables.
- **Resource Allocation:** Competing priorities and resource allocation decisions affecting project progress.

6. External Risks:

- **Market and Competitive:** Changes in market conditions or competitive landscape affecting project viability.
- **Legal and Compliance:** Risks related to legal requirements, regulations, or intellectual property rights.
- **Vendor and Supplier:** Risks associated with dependencies on external vendors or suppliers for components or services.

7. Environmental Risks:

- **Infrastructure:** Risks related to infrastructure failures, network disruptions, or environmental factors impacting project continuity.
- **Natural Disasters:** Potential disruptions caused by natural disasters or unforeseen events.

Managing Risks:

- **Identification:** Systematic identification of risks through brainstorming, expert judgment, and historical data analysis.
- **Assessment:** Evaluating risks based on likelihood, impact, and detectability to prioritize mitigation efforts.
- **Mitigation:** Developing and implementing strategies to reduce the probability and/or impact of risks.
- **Monitoring and Control:** Continuously monitoring risks throughout the project lifecycle, updating risk assessments, and implementing contingency plans as needed.

By addressing the diverse nature of risks in software project management proactively, project teams can enhance project predictability, mitigate potential disruptions, and increase the likelihood of successful project outcomes.

3.10 Types of Risks

In software project management, risks can be categorized into several types based on their nature, impact, and origin. Here are the common types of risks that project managers need to consider and manage during activity planning:

1. Technical Risks:

- **Technology Complexity:** Challenges arising from the complexity of the technology stack, including integration issues, scalability concerns, or unfamiliarity with new tools or frameworks.
- **Performance Risks:** Risks related to meeting performance requirements under expected and peak loads, including response times, throughput, and system stability.
- **Security Risks:** Concerns about vulnerabilities, data breaches, or inadequate security measures that could compromise the integrity and confidentiality of the software.

2. Requirements and Scope Risks:

- **Incomplete or Unclear Requirements:** Ambiguities, inconsistencies, or changing requirements that lead to misunderstandings, rework, and scope creep.
- **Scope Creep:** Gradual expansion of project scope beyond initial agreements, impacting schedule, resources, and project objectives.
- **Requirements Volatility:** Unforeseen changes in requirements during the project lifecycle, necessitating adjustments in plans and schedules.

3. Schedule Risks:

- **Estimation Risks:** Errors or inaccuracies in estimating task durations, dependencies, and overall project timelines.
- **Dependency Risks:** Delays caused by dependencies on external factors, third-party deliverables, or interdependent tasks.
- **Resource Constraints:** Shortages or fluctuations in availability of key resources (e.g., skilled personnel, equipment) affecting project progress.

4. Quality Risks:

- **Testing Risks:** Insufficient testing coverage, ineffective test strategies, or inadequate testing environments leading to undetected defects and poor software quality.
- **Defect Risks:** Potential for software defects impacting functionality, performance, reliability, and user experience.
- **Maintainability Risks:** Challenges related to the ease of maintaining and evolving the software post-deployment, including code complexity and documentation gaps.

5. Organizational Risks:

- **Team Dynamics:** Issues related to team collaboration, communication breakdowns, conflicting priorities, or skill gaps affecting productivity and morale.
- **Stakeholder Management:** Risks associated with managing diverse stakeholder expectations, conflicting interests, or changes in leadership.

- **Governance and Decision-Making:** Risks stemming from ineffective project governance structures, decision-making processes, or lack of clear roles and responsibilities.

6. External Risks:

- **Market Risks:** Changes in market conditions, customer preferences, competitive landscape, or regulatory requirements impacting project goals and outcomes.
- **Vendor and Supplier Risks:** Dependencies on external vendors, suppliers, or contractors for critical components, services, or expertise.
- **Legal and Compliance Risks:** Risks related to legal obligations, intellectual property rights, data privacy regulations, and contractual agreements.

7. Environmental Risks:

- **Infrastructure Risks:** Risks associated with infrastructure failures, network outages, power disruptions, or environmental factors (e.g., natural disasters) impacting project continuity.
- **Geopolitical Risks:** Risks arising from political instability, trade disputes, or international conflicts affecting project operations and delivery timelines.

Managing Risks:

Effective risk management in software project management involves:

- **Identification:** Systematic identification of potential risks through brainstorming, risk workshops, expert judgment, and historical data analysis.
- **Assessment:** Evaluating risks based on likelihood, impact, and detectability to prioritize them for mitigation efforts.
- **Mitigation:** Developing and implementing risk response strategies (e.g., avoidance, mitigation, transfer, acceptance) to reduce the probability and/or impact of risks.
- **Monitoring and Control:** Continuously monitoring identified risks throughout the project lifecycle, updating risk assessments, and implementing contingency plans as necessary.

By addressing these types of risks proactively during activity planning, project teams can enhance project predictability, minimize disruptions, and increase the likelihood of achieving project objectives within scope, schedule, and budget constraints.

3.11 Managing Risk

Managing risk in software project management involves a systematic approach to identifying, assessing, prioritizing, and mitigating potential risks that could impact project success. Here's a structured framework for managing risks during activity planning:

1. Risk Identification:

- **Brainstorming and Workshops:** Engage project stakeholders, team members, and subject matter experts to identify potential risks.

- **Checklists and Templates:** Use historical data, lessons learned, and risk checklists to systematically identify common risks in software projects (e.g., requirements volatility, technical complexity).
- **Documentation Review:** Review project documentation, requirements documents, and project plans to uncover potential risks.

2. Risk Assessment:

- **Probability and Impact Analysis:** Assess the likelihood of each identified risk occurring and its potential impact on project objectives (e.g., schedule, cost, quality).
- **Risk Categorization:** Classify risks into categories (e.g., technical, organizational, external) to prioritize mitigation efforts.
- **Risk Ranking:** Prioritize risks based on a combined assessment of their probability and impact using techniques like risk matrices or qualitative assessments.

3. Risk Mitigation Strategies:

- **Avoidance:** Modify the project plan to eliminate the risk or adjust activities to reduce exposure to the risk.
- **Mitigation:** Implement proactive measures to reduce the probability or impact of risks. This may involve actions such as conducting feasibility studies, prototyping, or improving communication.
- **Transfer:** Shift the risk to third parties, such as through outsourcing or insurance, if feasible and cost-effective.
- **Acceptance:** Acknowledge the risk and prepare contingency plans to mitigate its impact if it materializes, particularly for risks with low probability or impact.

4. Developing Contingency Plans:

- **Contingency Planning:** Develop contingency plans for high-priority risks to outline specific actions that will be taken if the risk occurs.
- **Fallback Plans:** Prepare alternative strategies or fallback plans to handle unforeseen events or scenarios that may arise during project execution.

5. Integrating Risk Management into Project Activities:

- **Embedding in Project Plans:** Integrate risk management activities into the overall project plan and schedule. Assign responsibilities for risk management tasks to team members or specific roles.
- **Regular Reviews:** Continuously monitor identified risks throughout the project lifecycle. Update risk assessments and response strategies as necessary based on changing circumstances or new information.
- **Communication:** Maintain open communication channels with stakeholders, ensuring they are informed about identified risks, mitigation efforts, and contingency plans.

6. Monitoring and Control:

- **Risk Tracking:** Use tools and techniques to track identified risks, monitor their status, and measure the effectiveness of mitigation actions.

- **Risk Reviews:** Conduct regular risk reviews during project meetings or checkpoints to assess the current status of identified risks and adjust mitigation strategies as needed.
- **Lessons Learned:** Document lessons learned from managing risks throughout the project to improve risk management practices in future projects.

Example Scenario:

In a software development project, consider a risk where there is a dependency on a third-party vendor for a critical component. The risk management approach would involve:

- **Identification:** Recognizing the dependency on the third-party vendor and potential risks associated with their delivery timelines or product quality.
- **Assessment:** Evaluating the probability of delays or quality issues from the vendor and the potential impact on project schedule and functionality.
- **Mitigation:** Developing a contingency plan that includes identifying alternative vendors, establishing clear communication channels with the current vendor, and possibly prototyping or conducting early testing to mitigate integration risks.
- **Monitoring and Control:** Continuously monitoring the vendor's progress and maintaining contingency plans to ensure timely responses if risks materialize.

By systematically managing risks during activity planning, software project managers can enhance project predictability, reduce uncertainty, and increase the likelihood of delivering projects on time, within budget, and meeting stakeholder expectations.

3.12 Hazard Identification

In software project management, hazard identification refers to the process of identifying potential hazards or risks that could adversely affect project objectives, such as schedule, budget, quality, and scope. While hazards are typically associated with physical environments, in the context of software projects, they can manifest as risks that may disrupt or delay project activities. Here's how hazard identification can be approached in activity planning:

1. Understanding Hazards in Software Projects:

- **Definition:** In software projects, hazards can be understood as potential risks that could lead to negative consequences, such as project delays, budget overruns, or quality issues.
- **Examples:**
    - **Technical Risks:** Issues with software development tools, libraries, or technologies that may cause delays or compatibility problems.
    - **Operational Risks:** Problems with project management tools, communication channels, or infrastructure failures that could disrupt workflow.
    - **External Risks:** Market changes, legal requirements, or vendor failures impacting project timelines and deliverables.

2. Methods for Hazard Identification:

- **Brainstorming:** Engage project stakeholders, team members, and subject matter experts to identify potential hazards based on their experience and knowledge of the project environment.
- **Checklists and Templates:** Use predefined checklists, historical data, lessons learned from previous projects, and risk management templates to systematically identify common hazards.
- **Documentation Review:** Review project documentation, requirements documents, project plans, and external dependencies to uncover potential hazards that could impact project activities.

3. Steps in Hazard Identification:

- **Identify Potential Hazards:** List down all potential hazards that could affect the project's objectives.
- **Evaluate and Prioritize:** Assess each identified hazard based on its likelihood of occurrence and potential impact on the project.
- **Document Hazards:** Document identified hazards along with their characteristics, potential consequences, and initial assessment.

4. Example Scenario:

Suppose a software project involves integrating a third-party API for a critical feature. Hazards could include:

- **Technical Risks:** Unforeseen compatibility issues between the API and existing software components.
- **Operational Risks:** Delays in API documentation availability or insufficient technical support from the API provider.
- **External Risks:** Changes in the API provider's terms of service or discontinuation of support for the API.

5. Integration with Activity Planning:

- **Mitigation Strategies:** Develop risk response strategies to mitigate identified hazards. For instance, conduct thorough testing and validation of the API integration early in the project lifecycle.
- **Contingency Plans:** Prepare contingency plans to address potential disruptions caused by hazards, such as identifying alternative APIs or building fallback mechanisms.
- **Continuous Monitoring:** Regularly monitor identified hazards throughout the project lifecycle. Update risk assessments and response strategies as necessary based on changing circumstances or new information.

6. Communication and Collaboration:

- **Stakeholder Engagement:** Maintain open communication channels with stakeholders to ensure they are aware of identified hazards, mitigation efforts, and contingency plans.

By systematically identifying and addressing hazards in software project management, project teams can enhance project resilience, reduce uncertainty, and improve the likelihood of successful project outcomes within scope, schedule, and budget constraints.

3.13 Hazard Analysis

In software project management, hazard analysis refers to the systematic process of identifying, assessing, and mitigating potential hazards or risks that could impact project objectives. It involves identifying the root causes of risks and determining appropriate measures to manage or eliminate them. Here's how hazard analysis is typically conducted in activity planning:

1. **Methods of Hazard Analysis:**

a. **Failure Mode and Effect Analysis (FMEA):**

- **Definition:** FMEA is a structured approach to identify potential failure modes of a system, software, or process, and their effects on project objectives.
- **Steps:**
    1. **Identify Failure Modes:** List possible failure modes or ways in which the software or project activities could fail.
    2. **Assess Severity:** Evaluate the severity of each failure mode's potential impact on project objectives (e.g., schedule, quality).
    3. **Determine Probability:** Assess the likelihood of each failure mode occurring.
    4. **Detect ability:** Evaluate how easily each failure mode can be detected before it causes harm.
    5. **Prioritize Risks:** Calculate a risk priority number (RPN) by multiplying severity, probability, and detect ability scores to prioritize risks for mitigation.

b. **Fault Tree Analysis (FTA):**

- **Definition:** FTA is a deductive approach that starts with an undesired event (top event) and analyzes its potential causes (faults) using a tree-like diagram.
- **Steps:**
    1. **Define Top Event:** Identify the undesired event or hazard that needs to be prevented.
    2. **Identify Basic Events:** Break down the top event into its contributing basic events or causes.
    3. **Analyze Causes:** Determine how each basic event contributes to the occurrence of the top event.
    4. **Assess Probability:** Evaluate the probability of each basic event occurring.
    5. **Mitigation Strategies:** Develop mitigation strategies based on the analysis to prevent or reduce the likelihood of the top event.

c. **Hazard and Operability Study (HAZOP):**

- **Definition:** HAZOP is a systematic technique used to identify potential hazards and operability issues in systems, processes, or software.
- **Steps:**
    1. **Select Parameters:** Identify critical parameters (e.g., inputs, conditions) of the system or software being analyzed.
    2. **Deviate Parameters:** Systematically vary each parameter to explore potential deviations or abnormal conditions.
    3. **Identify Hazards:** Identify potential hazards or consequences resulting from each parameter deviation.
    4. **Assess Risks:** Evaluate the severity and likelihood of each identified hazard.
    5. **Recommend Controls:** Recommend control measures or modifications to prevent or mitigate identified hazards.

2. **Integrating Hazard Analysis into Activity Planning:**
    - **Early Stage Analysis:** Conduct hazard analysis during the early stages of project planning and design to proactively identify and address risks.
    - **Iterative Process:** Continuously update and refine hazard analysis throughout the project lifecycle as new risks emerge or project conditions change.
    - **Documentation:** Document findings, risk assessments, and mitigation strategies to ensure clarity and accountability.
3. **Benefits of Hazard Analysis:**
    - **Risk Reduction:** Helps identify and mitigate potential hazards before they impact project objectives.
    - **Improved Decision Making:** Provides data-driven insights for making informed decisions on risk management strategies.
    - **Enhanced Project Resilience:** Increases project resilience by addressing potential risks early and implementing effective mitigation measures.

Example Scenario:

In a software development project, conducting a hazard analysis using FMEA might involve:

- **Identifying Failure Modes:** Potential failure modes could include software bugs, integration issues, or data security breaches.
- **Assessing Severity:** Evaluating the impact of each failure mode on project objectives, such as schedule delays or compromised data integrity.
- **Determining Probability:** Assessing the likelihood of each failure mode occurring based on historical data or expert judgment.
- **Mitigation Strategies:** Developing strategies like thorough testing, code reviews, and security audits to mitigate identified risks.

By incorporating robust hazard analysis techniques into activity planning, software project managers can effectively manage risks, enhance project predictability, and increase the likelihood of delivering successful projects within scope, schedule, and budget constraints.

3.14 Risk Planning and Control

Risk planning and control are integral parts of software project management activity planning. These processes involve identifying potential risks, analyzing their impacts, developing strategies to manage or mitigate them, and monitoring their progress throughout the project lifecycle. Here's how risk planning and control are typically executed:

1. Risk Planning:

a. **Risk Identification:**

- **Methods:** Use brainstorming sessions, checklists, historical data, and expert judgment to identify potential risks.
- **Documentation:** Document identified risks, their characteristics, and initial assessments.

b. **Risk Assessment:**

- **Risk Analysis Techniques:** Utilize qualitative (e.g., probability-impact matrix) and quantitative (e.g., Monte Carlo simulation) techniques to assess risks.
- **Prioritization:** Rank risks based on their impact on project objectives and likelihood of occurrence.

c. **Risk Response Planning:**

- **Strategies:** Develop risk response strategies for each identified risk:
    - **Avoidance:** Change project plans to eliminate the risk entirely.
    - **Mitigation:** Implement actions to reduce the probability or impact of the risk.
    - **Transfer:** Shift the risk to a third party, such as through insurance or outsourcing.
    - **Acceptance:** Acknowledge the risk without taking proactive measures unless it materializes.
- **Contingency Planning:** Develop contingency plans for high-priority risks to outline specific actions if they occur.

2. Risk Control:

a. **Implementation of Risk Responses:**

- **Execution:** Implement the planned risk response strategies effectively.
- **Monitoring:** Continuously monitor the effectiveness of implemented strategies in mitigating risks.

b. **Risk Reviews:**

- **Regular Reviews:** Conduct regular reviews of identified risks throughout the project lifecycle.
- **Updates:** Update risk assessments and response strategies based on changes in project conditions or new information.

c. **Risk Reporting and Communication:**

- **Stakeholder Communication:** Communicate risks, mitigation efforts, and contingency plans to stakeholders regularly.
- **Transparency:** Ensure transparency in reporting risks and their potential impacts on project outcomes.

d. **Adaptation and Adjustment:**

- **Iterative Process:** Adapt risk management strategies iteratively as the project progresses and new risks emerge.
- **Lessons Learned:** Document lessons learned from managing risks to improve risk management practices in future projects.

Example Scenario:

In a software development project:

- **Risk Planning:** Identify risks such as scope changes, technical uncertainties, and resource constraints.
  - **Risk Assessment:** Assess the impact of scope changes on project schedule and budget, evaluate technical risks related to new technology adoption, and analyze resource availability risks.
  - **Risk Response Planning:** Develop strategies such as frequent stakeholder communication to manage scope changes, conduct feasibility studies to mitigate technical uncertainties, and allocate backup resources to address potential resource constraints.
- **Risk Control:** Implement planned risk response strategies, monitor their effectiveness through regular reviews, and update risk assessments based on project progress and new risks identified.

By effectively planning for and controlling risks in software project management, project teams can enhance project predictability, minimize disruptions, and increase the likelihood of achieving project objectives within scope, schedule, and budget constraints.

Chapter 4

MONITORING AND CONTROL

Monitoring and control in software project management are crucial processes that ensure projects stay on track, meet objectives, and deliver expected outcomes. Here's an in-depth look at how these aspects are managed in software project management:

1. Monitoring in Software Project Management:

Monitoring involves tracking project activities, progress, and performance metrics against the project plan and baseline. Key aspects of monitoring include:

- **Progress Tracking:** Regularly monitor the status of tasks, milestones, and deliverables to ensure they are completed on schedule.
- **Quality Assurance:** Monitor the quality of deliverables through reviews, testing, and validation processes to meet defined standards.
- **Resource Utilization:** Monitor the allocation and usage of resources (e.g., personnel, equipment, budget) to optimize efficiency and prevent overruns.
- **Risk Monitoring:** Continuously assess and monitor identified risks, including their likelihood and impact on project objectives.
- **Communication:** Maintain open communication channels to keep stakeholders informed about project progress, issues, and changes.

2. Control in Software Project Management:

Control involves taking corrective actions to address deviations from the project plan and ensuring that project objectives are achieved. Key aspects of control include:

- **Change Management:** Implement formal processes to assess, approve, and manage changes to project scope, schedule, or resources.
- **Issue Resolution:** Identify and address issues promptly to minimize their impact on project progress and outcomes.
- **Risk Management:** Execute risk response plans to mitigate risks and manage unexpected events that may affect project success.
- **Performance Management:** Evaluate performance against key performance indicators (KPIs) and take corrective actions as needed to maintain project alignment with goals.
- **Quality Control:** Monitor and verify that project deliverables meet quality standards and requirements.

3. Tools and Techniques for Monitoring and Control:

- **Project Management Software:** Utilize tools such as Microsoft Project, Jira, or Trello for scheduling, task management, and collaboration.
- **Metrics and Dashboards:** Develop and maintain metrics dashboards to provide real-time visibility into project status, progress, and performance.
- **Regular Reviews and Meetings:** Conduct regular project reviews, status meetings, and checkpoints to discuss progress, issues, and action plans.
- **Earned Value Management (EVM):** Use EVM techniques to assess project performance against the planned budget and schedule.

4. Steps in Monitoring and Control:

- **Establish Baselines:** Define project baselines for scope, schedule, budget, and quality against which performance will be measured.
- **Monitor Performance:** Track actual performance metrics and compare them against the baselines to identify variances.
- **Analyze Deviations:** Analyze the causes of deviations and assess their potential impact on project objectives.
- **Take Corrective Actions:** Implement corrective actions to address deviations, mitigate risks, and ensure project alignment with goals.
- **Document and Communicate:** Document monitoring results, control actions taken, and communicate updates to stakeholders regularly.

Example Scenario:

In a software development project:

- **Monitoring:** Track progress of development tasks, conduct regular code reviews and testing to ensure quality, monitor resource usage, and assess risks related to technology dependencies.
- **Control:** Address issues such as scope changes through change control procedures, mitigate risks identified during testing, adjust resource allocations based on project needs, and manage stakeholder expectations through effective communication.

By effectively managing monitoring and control processes in software project management, teams can enhance project transparency, mitigate risks proactively, optimize resources, and increase the likelihood of delivering projects successfully within scope, schedule, and budget constraints.

4.1 Creating Framework

Creating a framework for monitoring and controlling software projects involves establishing structured processes and tools to track project progress, manage risks, and ensure adherence to project plans. Here's a comprehensive framework for monitoring and control in software project management:

1. Define Project Objectives and Metrics:

- **Clarity:** Clearly define project objectives, deliverables, milestones, and success criteria.
- **Metrics:** Establish key performance indicators (KPIs) to measure progress and performance (e.g., schedule adherence, budget variance, quality metrics).

2. Establish Baselines:

- **Baseline Plans:** Develop baseline schedules, budgets, and scope documents against which actual performance will be measured.
- **Configuration Management:** Implement configuration management processes to manage changes to project baselines.

3. Implement Monitoring Processes:

- **Progress Tracking:** Regularly monitor and update progress against the baseline plans.
- **Issue Identification:** Continuously identify and document issues, risks, and deviations from planned activities.
- **Performance Reviews:** Conduct periodic performance reviews to assess project health and identify areas needing improvement.

4. Risk Management:

- **Identify Risks:** Continuously identify and assess risks throughout the project lifecycle.
- **Mitigation Strategies:** Develop and implement risk response plans to minimize the impact of identified risks.
- **Risk Reviews:** Regularly review and update risk assessments based on changing project conditions.

5. Change Management:

- **Change Control Process:** Establish a formal change management process to assess, approve, and implement changes to project scope, schedule, or resources.
- **Impact Assessment:** Evaluate the impact of proposed changes on project objectives and adjust plans accordingly.

6. Communication and Reporting:

- **Stakeholder Communication:** Maintain open communication channels with stakeholders to provide regular updates on project status, risks, and issues.
- **Reporting:** Prepare and distribute project status reports, dashboards, and performance metrics tailored to the needs of various stakeholders.

7. Quality Assurance:

- **Quality Reviews:** Conduct quality assurance reviews to ensure that deliverables meet predefined quality standards.
- **Testing and Validation:** Implement rigorous testing and validation processes to detect and address defects early in the development lifecycle.

8. Performance Improvement:

- **Lessons Learned:** Document and incorporate lessons learned from project activities to improve processes and avoid recurring issues.
- **Continuous Improvement:** Foster a culture of continuous improvement by regularly reviewing and refining project management practices.

9. Tool and Technology Integration:

- **Project Management Tools:** Utilize project management software and tools for scheduling, task management, issue tracking, and collaboration.
- **Metrics Dashboard:** Implement a centralized metrics dashboard to provide real-time visibility into project performance and health.

10. Review and Adaptation:

- **Regular Reviews:** Conduct periodic project reviews to evaluate the effectiveness of the monitoring and control framework.
- **Adaptation:** Modify and adapt the framework based on lessons learned, feedback from stakeholders, and changing project requirements.

Example Scenario:

In a software development project:

- **Framework Establishment:** Define project objectives, establish baseline plans for schedule and budget, and implement a change management process.
- **Monitoring and Control:** Monitor progress against baseline schedules, track budget expenditures, identify and mitigate risks, and manage changes through formal approval processes.
- **Communication:** Regularly communicate project status, risks, and issues to stakeholders through status reports and meetings.

- **Quality Assurance:** Conduct quality reviews and testing activities to ensure software meets quality standards before deployment.
- **Continuous Improvement:** Review project performance, document lessons learned, and incorporate feedback to enhance project management practices in future projects.

By creating and implementing a robust monitoring and control framework in software project management, project teams can effectively manage risks, optimize resources, and increase the likelihood of delivering projects on time, within budget, and meeting stakeholder expectations.

4.2 Collecting The Data

Collecting data in software project management monitoring and control involves gathering relevant information on project progress, performance metrics, risks, issues, and other critical aspects. Here's how data collection is typically managed:

1. Identifying Key Data Points:

- **Project Objectives:** Determine which data points align with project goals, such as schedule adherence, budget utilization, quality metrics, and scope changes.
- **Performance Indicators:** Define key performance indicators (KPIs) that reflect project health and progress, such as:
    - Schedule variance (SV)
    - Cost variance (CV)
    - Earned value (EV)
    - Quality metrics (defect density, testing coverage)
    - Resource utilization rates
- **Risk Metrics:** Identify metrics related to risk management, such as number of identified risks, risk severity levels, and effectiveness of risk response actions.

2. Sources of Data:

- **Project Management Tools:** Utilize software tools like Microsoft Project, Jira, Trello, or Asana for task tracking, scheduling, and collaboration.
- **Time Tracking Systems:** Capture data on time spent by team members on specific tasks or activities.
- **Financial Systems:** Extract data related to project budget allocations, expenditures, and financial forecasts.
- **Quality Assurance Tools:** Gather data from testing tools, code repositories, and quality assurance reports.
- **Risk Registers:** Document and update information on identified risks, their probabilities, impacts, and mitigation strategies.

3. Methods of Data Collection:

- **Automated Data Collection:** Utilize automated mechanisms within project management tools to capture real-time data on task progress, milestones achieved, and resource usage.
- **Manual Reporting:** Regularly collect and update data through manual reporting processes, such as team status updates, progress reports, and risk assessments.
- **Surveys and Interviews:** Conduct surveys or interviews with team members, stakeholders, and subject matter experts to gather qualitative data on project performance, issues, and concerns.
- **Document Reviews:** Analyze project documentation, meeting minutes, and change requests to gather relevant information on project status and changes.

4. Data Collection Practices:

- **Consistency:** Establish consistent data collection practices to ensure accuracy and reliability of collected information.
- **Timeliness:** Collect data at regular intervals or milestones to provide up-to-date insights into project progress and performance.
- **Accuracy:** Validate data for accuracy and completeness, addressing any discrepancies or inconsistencies promptly.
- **Security:** Ensure data security and confidentiality, especially when handling sensitive information related to project finances, risks, or proprietary technologies.

5. Data Analysis and Reporting:

- **Analysis:** Analyze collected data to identify trends, patterns, and deviations from planned objectives.
- **Reporting:** Prepare and distribute reports, dashboards, or visualizations that summarize project performance, risks, issues, and recommended actions to stakeholders.
- **Communication:** Communicate findings and insights effectively to stakeholders, facilitating informed decision-making and proactive management of project challenges.

Example Scenario:

In a software development project:

- **Data Points:** Collect data on task completion rates, budget expenditures, testing outcomes (defects found and resolved), and risks identified.
- **Sources:** Utilize Jira for task tracking, financial systems for budget data, quality assurance tools for testing metrics, and risk registers for risk management data.

- **Methods:** Automate task progress updates through Jira workflows, manually collect budget and financial data from accounting systems, and conduct regular team meetings to gather qualitative insights.

By systematically collecting and analyzing relevant data in software project management, project teams can gain valuable insights into project performance, proactively manage risks and issues, and optimize decision-making to ensure successful project outcomes.

4.3 Visualizing Progress

Visualizing progress in software project management is essential for providing stakeholders with clear, intuitive insights into project status, performance, and key metrics. Effective visualization enhances communication, facilitates decision-making, and promotes transparency throughout the project lifecycle. Here are several ways to visualize progress in software project management:

1. Gantt Charts:

- **Description:** Gantt charts visually represent project schedules, tasks, milestones, and dependencies over time.
- **Usage:** Show task progress, dependencies, and critical path to understand project timeline and identify potential delays.
- **Benefits:** Provides a comprehensive overview of project status and helps in scheduling and resource management.

2. Burn down Charts:

- **Description:** Burn down charts track the progress of work remaining against time.
- **Usage:** Show whether the project is on track to complete tasks within the planned timeframe.
- **Benefits:** Easily identify deviations from planned work rates and adjust resources or priorities accordingly.

3. Earned Value Management (EVM) Charts:

- **Description:** EVM charts integrate project scope, schedule, and cost measures.
- **Usage:** Compare planned vs. actual progress in terms of cost and schedule performance.
- **Benefits:** Provides insights into cost and schedule variances and forecasts project completion dates and costs.

4. Kanban Boards:

- **Description:** Kanban boards visualize tasks in different stages of completion (e.g., to do, in progress, done).
- **Usage:** Track task status, identify bottlenecks, and manage workflow efficiently.
- **Benefits:** Facilitates real-time collaboration and allows teams to prioritize tasks effectively.

5. Dashboard and Metrics Visualization:

- **Description:** Dashboards integrate various project metrics and KPIs into a single visual interface.
- **Usage:** Provide a holistic view of project health, including progress, risks, quality metrics, and resource utilization.
- **Benefits:** Enables stakeholders to quickly grasp project performance trends, make informed decisions, and take timely actions.

6. Quality Metrics and Defect Charts:

- **Description:** Visualize quality metrics such as defect density, severity levels, and test coverage.
- **Usage:** Track software quality and identify areas requiring improvement.
- **Benefits:** Improve decision-making related to release readiness and identify patterns in defects for proactive mitigation.

7. Risk Heat maps:

- **Description:** Risk heat maps visually represent risks based on their likelihood and impact.
- **Usage:** Prioritize risks for mitigation efforts and communicate risk exposure to stakeholders.
- **Benefits:** Facilitates risk management by highlighting critical risks and their potential consequences.

8. Team Velocity Charts:

- **Description:** Team velocity charts track the amount of work completed by a team over iterations or sprints.
- **Usage:** Assess team productivity and predict future performance based on historical data.
- **Benefits:** Helps in capacity planning and optimizing team resources.

Best Practices for Visualizing Progress:

- **Tailor to Audience:** Customize visuals based on stakeholder needs and preferences (e.g., high-level summaries for executives, detailed metrics for project teams).
- **Real-Time Updates:** Ensure visuals are updated regularly to reflect the latest project data and status.
- **Clear Annotations:** Provide clear labels, annotations, and legends to enhance understanding and interpretation of visuals.
- **Interactive Features:** Use interactive features where applicable to allow stakeholders to drill down into details or adjust parameters.
- **Consistency:** Maintain consistency in visualization formats and metrics to facilitate comparison over time and across projects.

Visualizing progress in software project management not only enhances communication and decision-making but also fosters collaboration and accountability among project stakeholders. By using appropriate visualization techniques, project teams can effectively monitor and control projects, mitigate risks, and ensure successful project delivery within scope, schedule, and budget constraints.

4.4 Cost Monitoring

Cost monitoring in software project management is crucial to ensure projects stay within budget constraints and financial resources are effectively managed. Here's how cost monitoring is typically conducted:

1. Establishing Cost Baselines:

- **Baseline Definition:** Define initial estimates and budgets for the project, including costs for resources, equipment, software licenses, and other expenses.
- **Budget Allocation:** Allocate funds across different phases or activities of the project based on the project plan and requirements.

2. Tracking Actual Costs:

- **Expense Tracking:** Monitor actual expenditures incurred during the project lifecycle.
- **Time Tracking:** Track labor costs by recording hours worked by team members and their associated rates.

3. Cost Performance Metrics:

- **Cost Variance (CV):** Calculate the difference between earned value (EV) and actual costs (AC).

$$CV = EV - AC.$$

- **Schedule Variance (SV):** Measure the difference between earned value (EV) and planned value (PV).

$$SV = EV - PV.$$

- **Cost Performance Index (CPI):** Measure the efficiency of cost performance relative to the budget.

$$CPI = EV / AC.$$

- **Estimate at Completion (EAC):** Forecast the total cost of the project based on current performance.

$$EAC = AC + (BAC - EV).$$

4. Tools and Techniques:

- **Project Management Software:** Use tools like Microsoft Project, Primavera, or Open Project to track and manage project costs.
- **Timesheets and Expense Reports:** Collect data through timesheets, expense reports, and financial systems to accurately track costs.

5. Cost Control Actions:

- **Monitoring Thresholds:** Set thresholds for cost variances and CPI to trigger reviews and corrective actions.
- **Change Management:** Manage changes to scope, schedule, or resources through formal change control processes to prevent cost overruns.
- **Resource Allocation:** Optimize resource allocation based on cost performance metrics to maximize efficiency and minimize costs.

6. Reporting and Communication:

- **Cost Reports:** Generate regular cost reports and dashboards to communicate project financial status to stakeholders.
- **Variance Analysis:** Conduct variance analysis to explain deviations from the budget and propose corrective actions.

Example Scenario:

In a software development project:

- **Baseline:** Establish a baseline budget for hardware, software licenses, development resources, and other project expenses.

- **Tracking:** Use project management software to track actual expenditures against the baseline budget, including labor costs and material expenses.
- **Metrics:** Calculate CV, SV, CPI, and EAC regularly to assess cost performance and predict final project costs.
- **Actions:** Implement cost control measures such as adjusting resource allocations, reviewing scope changes, or renegotiating vendor contracts based on cost performance metrics.

By effectively monitoring and controlling costs in software project management, teams can optimize financial resources, identify potential issues early, and maintain project profitability while delivering within scope, schedule, and quality expectations.

4.5 Earned Value Analysis

Earned Value Analysis (EVA) is a powerful technique used in software project management for monitoring and controlling project performance. It integrates measurements of scope, schedule, and cost to assess project progress and forecast future performance. Here's an overview of how Earned Value Analysis works and its key components:

Components of Earned Value Analysis:

1. **Planned Value (PV):**
    - **Definition:** Also known as Budgeted Cost of Work Scheduled (BCWS), PV represents the authorized budget assigned to the scheduled work to be accomplished by a specific point in time.
    - **Purpose:** PV establishes the baseline against which actual performance is measured in terms of cost.
2. **Earned Value (EV):**
    - **Definition:** Also known as Budgeted Cost of Work Performed (BCWP), EV represents the value of the work actually completed at a specific point in time.
    - **Measurement:** EV is typically measured in monetary terms based on the completion of scheduled tasks or milestones.
3. **Actual Cost (AC):**
    - **Definition:** Also known as Actual Cost of Work Performed (ACWP), AC represents the actual costs incurred for the work performed up to a specific point in time.
    - **Measurement:** AC includes all costs, such as labor, materials, equipment, and overheads.

Key Metrics Derived from Earned Value Analysis:

1. **Cost Variance (CV):**
   - **Formula:** CV = EV - AC
   - **Interpretation:** CV indicates whether the project is under budget (positive CV) or over budget (negative CV) at the time of measurement.
2. **Schedule Variance (SV):**
   - **Formula:** SV = EV - PV
   - **Interpretation:** SV indicates whether the project is ahead of schedule (positive SV) or behind schedule (negative SV) at the time of measurement.
3. **Cost Performance Index (CPI):**
   - **Formula:** CPI = EV / AC
   - **Interpretation:** CPI measures the efficiency of cost performance relative to the budget. $CPI > 1$ indicates costs are under budget, $CPI < 1$ indicates costs are over budget.
4. **Schedule Performance Index (SPI):**
   - **Formula:** SPI = EV / PV
   - **Interpretation:** SPI measures the efficiency of schedule performance relative to the baseline schedule. $SPI > 1$ indicates the project is ahead of schedule, $SPI < 1$ indicates the project is behind schedule.
5. **Estimate at Completion (EAC):**
   - **Formula:** EAC = AC + (BAC - EV)
   - **Interpretation:** EAC forecasts the total project cost based on current performance. There are several methods to calculate EAC depending on assumptions about future performance.

Application of Earned Value Analysis in Software Project Management:

- **Performance Measurement:** EVA provides objective measures of project performance in terms of cost and schedule, allowing project managers to identify variances early.
- **Forecasting:** EVA enables forecasting of total project costs and completion dates based on current performance trends, helping in proactive management.
- **Decision Making:** By analyzing CV, SV, CPI, and SPI, project managers can make informed decisions regarding resource allocation, risk management, and corrective actions.

Example Scenario:

In a software development project:

- **PV:** The planned budget for completing a software module by a specific date is $50,000.

- **EV:** Upon assessment, it is determined that the actual work completed by that date is valued at $45,000.
- **AC:** The actual cost incurred for completing the work is $48,000.

Based on these values:

- **CV:** CV = EV - AC = $45,000 - $48,000 = -$3,000 (over budget)
- **SV:** SV = EV - PV = $45,000 - $50,000 = -$5,000 (behind schedule)
- **CPI:** CPI = EV / AC = $45,000 / $48,000 = 0.9375 (cost efficiency less than 1 indicates over budget)
- **SPI:** SPI = EV / PV = $45,000 / $50,000 = 0.9 (schedule efficiency less than 1 indicates behind schedule)
- **EAC:** EAC = AC + (BAC - EV) = $48,000 + ($50,000 - $45,000) = $53,000 (forecasted total project cost based on current performance)

By leveraging Earned Value Analysis, project managers can proactively manage software projects, identify potential issues early, and take corrective actions to ensure projects are delivered within scope, schedule, and budget constraints.

4.6 Prioritizing Monitoring

Prioritizing monitoring activities in software project management ensures that resources are allocated effectively, risks are managed proactively, and project goals are achieved efficiently. Here are key areas to prioritize in monitoring and controlling software projects:

1. Schedule and Milestone Tracking:

- **Importance:** Monitoring schedule adherence helps ensure timely delivery of project milestones and overall completion.
- **Activities:**
  - Regularly update and review Gantt charts or project schedules.
  - Track progress against planned milestones and critical path activities.
  - Identify and address schedule deviations promptly to prevent delays.

2. Budget and Cost Management:

- **Importance:** Monitoring costs ensures that the project stays within budgetary constraints and financial resources are optimally utilized.
- **Activities:**
  - Track actual costs versus budgeted costs (Earned Value Analysis).
  - Monitor cost variances (CV) and cost performance index (CPI).

- Implement cost control measures based on variances to prevent overruns.

3. Quality Assurance and Testing:

- **Importance:** Monitoring quality ensures that deliverables meet specified requirements and standards, reducing rework and ensuring customer satisfaction.
- **Activities:**
  - Conduct regular quality inspections and reviews.
  - Track defect rates, severity, and resolution progress.
  - Monitor testing coverage and effectiveness of test cases.

4. Risk Management:

- **Importance:** Monitoring risks allows for early identification and mitigation of potential issues that could impact project objectives.
- **Activities:**
  - Regularly update the risk register with new risks and reassess existing risks.
  - Monitor risk triggers and early warning indicators.
  - Implement risk response actions and contingency plans as necessary.

5. Resource Allocation and Utilization:

- **Importance:** Monitoring resource allocation ensures that human and material resources are effectively utilized to maximize productivity.
- **Activities:**
  - Track resource availability and workload.
  - Monitor resource utilization rates and productivity metrics.
  - Adjust resource allocations based on project needs and performance data.

6. Stakeholder Communication:

- **Importance:** Regular communication with stakeholders ensures alignment of expectations, facilitates decision-making, and addresses concerns promptly.
- **Activities:**
  - Schedule regular status meetings and updates.
  - Provide transparent and accurate project reports and dashboards.
  - Address stakeholder feedback and incorporate changes as necessary.

7. Change Management:

- **Importance:** Monitoring changes helps in assessing their impact on project scope, schedule, and resources, ensuring controlled project evolution.
- **Activities:**
    - Maintain a formal change control process.
    - Assess change requests against project baselines and objectives.
    - Monitor the implementation and impact of approved changes.

8. Progress Reporting and Documentation:

- **Importance:** Regular reporting provides visibility into project status, progress, and performance metrics to stakeholders and project teams.
- **Activities:**
    - Prepare and distribute regular progress reports, dashboards, and metrics.
    - Document key decisions, actions taken, and lessons learned.
    - Ensure documentation is up-to-date and accessible to relevant stakeholders.

Prioritization Strategy:

- **Critical Path Analysis:** Identify activities on the critical path and prioritize monitoring efforts for these activities to avoid schedule delays.
- **Risk Impact and Probability:** Prioritize monitoring efforts for high-impact and high-probability risks to mitigate potential disruptions.
- **Stakeholder Needs:** Align monitoring activities with stakeholder expectations and priorities to ensure project success and stakeholder satisfaction.

By prioritizing these monitoring activities in software project management, teams can effectively manage project performance, minimize risks, and optimize resource utilization, ultimately ensuring successful project delivery within defined scope, schedule, and budget constraints.

4.7 Getting Project Back to Target

When a software project deviates from its target in terms of schedule, budget, or quality, it's crucial to take proactive steps to bring it back on track. Here's a structured approach to getting a project back to its target in software project management:

1. Assess the Current Situation:

- **Gather Data:** Collect and analyze project performance data, including schedule progress, budget expenditures, quality metrics, and identified risks/issues.

- **Identify Deviations:** Determine the specific areas where the project has deviated from the original plan or target objectives.

2. Root Cause Analysis:

- **Identify Causes:** Conduct a root cause analysis to understand why the project has veered off course. Common reasons include scope changes, resource constraints, unrealistic estimates, technical challenges, or external dependencies.
- **Prioritize Issues:** Prioritize the identified issues based on their impact on project objectives and criticality to project success.

3. Develop Corrective Action Plan:

- **Set Clear Objectives:** Define specific, measurable objectives for bringing the project back to target (e.g., schedule adherence, cost containment, quality improvements).
- **Action Steps:** Outline concrete actions and strategies to address each identified issue. This may include revising the project plan, reallocating resources, adjusting schedules, or revisiting scope commitments.

4. Implement Corrective Actions:

- **Allocate Resources:** Ensure adequate resources (human, financial, technological) are allocated to execute the corrective action plan effectively.
- **Communicate Changes:** Communicate revised plans, expectations, and responsibilities to the project team and stakeholders.

5. Monitor Progress:

- **Track Performance:** Continuously monitor the implementation of corrective actions and measure progress against defined objectives.
- **Use Earned Value Analysis:** Utilize Earned Value Analysis (EVA) or other performance metrics to assess the effectiveness of corrective actions in realigning the project.

6. Manage Risks and Issues:

- **Proactively Address Risks:** Monitor and manage remaining risks and issues to prevent new deviations from occurring.
- **Adjust Plans:** Be prepared to adjust the corrective action plan based on evolving project conditions or new challenges that arise.

7. Engage Stakeholders:

- **Communicate Progress:** Provide regular updates to stakeholders on the status of corrective actions and their impact on project outcomes.
- **Seek Support:** Engage stakeholders for support in overcoming obstacles or securing additional resources if needed.

8. Continuous Improvement:

- **Learn from Lessons:** Document lessons learned from the corrective action process to improve future project planning and management practices.
- **Iterate as Necessary:** Iterate on the corrective action plan based on ongoing feedback and new insights gained during implementation.

Example Scenario:

Suppose a software development project is behind schedule due to unforeseen technical challenges and resource shortages. The project manager takes the following steps to bring the project back to its target:

- **Assessment:** Analyzes project schedule data and identifies critical path delays caused by technical issues.
- **Root Cause Analysis:** Determines that the delays stem from inadequate resource allocation and underestimated complexity of software modules.
- **Corrective Action Plan:** Develops a plan to reallocate additional resources to critical tasks, streamline development processes, and conduct targeted training to address technical gaps.
- **Implementation:** Executes the plan by adjusting resource assignments, improving communication among team members, and leveraging expertise from external consultants.
- **Monitoring:** Monitors progress through regular status meetings, tracking key performance indicators (KPIs), and adjusting plans based on updated data and feedback.

By following a structured approach to assessing, analyzing, and implementing corrective actions, software project managers can effectively mitigate deviations from project targets and ensure successful project completion within defined constraints.

4.8 Change Control

Change control in software project management refers to the process of managing changes to project scope, schedule, resources, and deliverables in a controlled and systematic manner. It ensures that changes are evaluated, approved, implemented, and monitored while minimizing disruptions and maintaining project integrity. Here's a detailed overview of change control in software project management:

Key Components of Change Control:

1. **Change Identification:**
    - **Definition:** Identify and document proposed changes to project scope, requirements, schedule, or resources.
    - **Sources:** Changes can originate from stakeholders, team members, regulatory requirements, or external factors.
2. **Change Request Documentation:**
    - **Capture Details:** Document the nature of the change, rationale, potential impact, and associated risks.
    - **Formal Submission:** Submit change requests using a standardized form or template for review and approval.
3. **Change Evaluation:**
    - **Impact Assessment:** Evaluate the potential effects of the change on project scope, schedule, resources, costs, and quality.
    - **Risk Analysis:** Assess risks associated with implementing the change and its impact on project objectives.
    - **Feasibility Study:** Determine the technical and operational feasibility of implementing the change within project constraints.
4. **Change Approval Process:**
    - **Authorization:** Obtain approval from the designated change control board (CCB), project sponsor, or other relevant stakeholders.
    - **Review Criteria:** Review change requests based on predefined criteria such as alignment with project objectives, benefits vs. costs, and impact on stakeholders.
5. **Change Implementation:**
    - **Plan Execution:** Develop an implementation plan detailing tasks, responsibilities, timelines, and resources required to implement the approved change.
    - **Communication:** Communicate approved changes to the project team and relevant stakeholders to ensure awareness and alignment.
6. **Change Monitoring and Control:**
    - **Tracking:** Monitor the execution of approved changes to ensure they are implemented as planned.
    - **Performance Evaluation:** Evaluate the impact of changes on project performance, schedule, budget, and quality.
    - **Documentation:** Update project documentation, including scope statements, requirements documents, and project plans, to reflect approved changes.

Best Practices for Effective Change Control:

- **Establish Clear Procedures:** Define and communicate formal procedures for submitting, evaluating, and approving change requests.
- **Use Change Control Boards (CCBs):** Form a CCB composed of key stakeholders to review and approve change requests based on established criteria.
- **Prioritize Changes:** Assess and prioritize change requests based on their impact, urgency, and alignment with project goals.
- **Document Everything:** Maintain comprehensive documentation of all change requests, evaluations, approvals, and implementation plans.
- **Communicate Effectively:** Ensure timely and transparent communication with stakeholders regarding the status of change requests and their implications.
- **Monitor and Review:** Regularly review and monitor the effectiveness of change control processes to identify areas for improvement.

Example Scenario:

In a software development project:

- **Change Request:** A stakeholder requests additional features to be added to the software product to enhance usability.
- **Evaluation:** The project team assesses the impact on project scope, resources, schedule, and budget. They conduct a feasibility study to determine if the changes can be accommodated without compromising the project's timeline and budget constraints.
- **Approval:** The change request is reviewed by the CCB, which evaluates the potential benefits, risks, and impacts on project objectives. After careful consideration, the CCB approves the change request.
- **Implementation:** The project manager develops an implementation plan, assigns tasks to the development team, and communicates the approved changes to stakeholders.
- **Monitoring:** Throughout the implementation phase, the project manager monitors progress, tracks resource usage, and ensures that the changes are integrated smoothly into the project.

By effectively managing change control in software project management, teams can adapt to evolving requirements, address stakeholder needs, and maintain project alignment with organizational goals while minimizing disruptions and maximizing project success.

4.9 Managing Contracts

Managing contracts in software project management involves overseeing agreements with vendors, subcontractors, and service providers to ensure that deliverables, timelines, costs, and quality expectations are met. Here are key aspects to consider when managing contracts in software project management:

1. Contract Planning:

- **Scope Definition:** Clearly define the scope of work, deliverables, and expectations in the contract. Specify software requirements, milestones, acceptance criteria, and project timelines.
- **Contract Types:** Determine the appropriate type of contract (e.g., fixed-price, time and materials, milestone-based) based on project requirements and risk tolerance.

2. Vendor Selection and Negotiation:

- **Vendor Assessment:** Evaluate potential vendors based on their expertise, track record, capabilities, and cost competitiveness.
- **Negotiation:** Negotiate contract terms, pricing, payment schedules, warranties, and service level agreements (SLAs) to ensure alignment with project needs and budget constraints.

3. Contract Administration:

- **Documentation:** Maintain accurate records of all contractual agreements, amendments, and correspondence throughout the project lifecycle.
- **Change Management:** Establish procedures for managing contract changes, including scope adjustments, budget revisions, and timeline extensions.
- **Compliance:** Ensure compliance with contractual obligations, regulatory requirements, and legal standards applicable to software development and procurement.

4. Performance Monitoring:

- **Metrics and KPIs:** Define performance metrics and key performance indicators (KPIs) to monitor vendor performance against contractual requirements.
- **Regular Reviews:** Conduct regular performance reviews and assessments to evaluate vendor deliverables, quality of work, adherence to schedules, and customer satisfaction.

5. Issue Resolution:

- **Escalation Procedures:** Establish escalation procedures to address contract disputes, issues, or disagreements promptly.
- **Mitigation Strategies:** Implement strategies to mitigate risks related to vendor performance, project delays, or quality deficiencies.

6. Financial Management:

- **Budget Control:** Monitor expenditures related to contracted services, track budget allocations, and manage financial risks associated with vendor payments.
- **Invoicing and Payments:** Verify vendor invoices for accuracy, completeness, and compliance with contract terms before processing payments.

7. Relationship Management:

- **Communication:** Foster open communication and collaboration with vendors to build strong working relationships.
- **Conflict Resolution:** Resolve conflicts and maintain positive vendor relationships through effective communication, negotiation, and problem-solving.

8. Contract Closure:

- **Completion Verification:** Verify that all contractual obligations, deliverables, and acceptance criteria have been met.
- **Documentation:** Ensure proper documentation of contract closure, including final acceptance, warranties, and release of liabilities.

Example Scenario:

In a software development project:

- **Contract Negotiation:** Negotiate a fixed-price contract with a software development firm to deliver a custom application within six months.
- **Performance Monitoring:** Monitor vendor progress through regular status meetings, milestone reviews, and testing phases to ensure adherence to project timelines and quality standards.
- **Issue Resolution:** Address scope changes requested by stakeholders through formal change requests, evaluating their impact on project scope, schedule, and budget.
- **Financial Management:** Track project expenditures against the contracted budget, ensuring that payments are made based on milestone achievements and deliverable acceptance criteria.

By effectively managing contracts in software project management, project teams can mitigate risks, ensure compliance with project requirements, and optimize vendor performance to achieve successful project outcomes within defined scope, schedule, and budget constraints

4.10 Types Of Contract

In software project management, various types of contracts can be used depending on project requirements, risk allocation preferences, and the relationship dynamics between the client and the vendor. Here are some common types of contracts used in software project management:

1. Fixed-Price Contract:

- **Description:** A fixed-price contract sets a predetermined price for the entire scope of work.
- **Characteristics:**
    - **Scope Clarity:** Requires well-defined project requirements and deliverables.
    - **Budget Certainty:** Provides predictability in costs for the client.
    - **Risk Allocation:** Places the risk of cost overruns on the vendor.
- **Usage:** Suitable when project requirements are stable and predictable, and scope changes are minimal.

2. Time and Materials (T&M) Contract:

- **Description:** A time and materials contract pays vendors based on the time spent and materials used.
- **Characteristics:**
    - **Flexibility:** Allows for flexibility in project scope and requirements.
    - **Cost Transparency:** Clients pay for actual hours worked and materials used.
    - **Risk Sharing:** Shares cost and schedule risks between the client and the vendor.
- **Usage:** Appropriate for projects with evolving requirements or where the scope is not fully defined initially.

3. Cost-Reimbursable Contract:

- **Description:** In a cost-reimbursable contract, the client reimburses the vendor for all allowable costs plus a fee.
- **Characteristics:**
    - **Cost Control:** Provides detailed visibility into project costs.
    - **Risk Allocation:** Transfers significant risk to the client.
    - **Flexibility:** Allows for changes in project scope and requirements.
- **Usage:** Used when the scope is uncertain or likely to change, and where the client wants control over project activities and costs.

4. Milestone-Based Contract:

- **Description:** Payments are tied to the achievement of specific milestones or deliverables.

- **Characteristics:**
    - **Performance-Based Payments:** Payments are linked to predefined milestones or project phases.
    - **Risk Mitigation:** Helps in managing project progress and ensuring deliverables meet quality standards.
- **Usage:** Suitable for projects with clear and measurable milestones, allowing for incremental payments as milestones are achieved.

5. Incentive-Based Contracts:

- **Description:** Incentive-based contracts include provisions for additional payments or penalties based on performance metrics.
- **Characteristics:**
    - **Performance Incentives:** Rewards vendors for exceeding performance targets.
    - **Penalties:** Imposes penalties for failing to meet agreed-upon performance metrics.
- **Usage:** Used to motivate vendors to achieve superior performance or to penalize underperformance.

6. Service Level Agreement (SLA):

- **Description:** SLAs define the level of service expected from the vendor, including quality, performance, and availability.
- **Characteristics:**
    - **Performance Metrics:** Includes measurable performance indicators (e.g., uptime, response time).
    - **Service Scope:** Defines the scope of services provided and the responsibilities of both parties.
- **Usage:** Often used in ongoing support and maintenance contracts to ensure service quality and performance standards are met.

Selection Considerations:

- **Project Complexity:** Choose a contract type that aligns with the project's complexity, uncertainty, and scope stability.
- **Risk Allocation:** Determine how risks related to cost overruns, schedule delays, and scope changes will be allocated between the client and the vendor.
- **Flexibility Requirements:** Assess the need for flexibility in project scope, requirements, and budget management.
- **Client-Vendor Relationship:** Consider the relationship dynamics and trust level between the client and the vendor when selecting the contract type.

By selecting the appropriate contract type in software project management, stakeholders can effectively manage project risks, control costs, and ensure alignment with project objectives and client expectations. Each type offers different advantages and considerations, depending on the specific needs and dynamics of the project

4.11 Stages In Contract Placement

In software project management, placing a contract involves several stages to ensure that the agreement between the client and vendor is well-defined, legally sound, and aligned with project objectives. Here are the key stages involved in contract placement:

1. Preparation and Planning:

- **Define Requirements:** Clearly define the project scope, objectives, deliverables, timelines, and quality expectations.
- **Identify Stakeholders:** Identify key stakeholders involved in the contract placement process, including project sponsors, legal advisors, procurement team members, and project managers.
- **Contract Strategy:** Determine the appropriate contract type (e.g., fixed-price, time and materials) based on project requirements, risk tolerance, and client-vendor relationship dynamics.

2. Solicitation and Vendor Selection:

- **Request for Proposals (RFP):** Prepare and issue an RFP document outlining project requirements, evaluation criteria, and submission guidelines.
- **Vendor Evaluation:** Evaluate vendor proposals based on criteria such as technical expertise, experience, cost, compliance with requirements, and references.
- **Negotiation:** Conduct negotiations with selected vendors regarding contract terms, pricing, payment schedules, scope adjustments, and service level agreements (SLAs).

3. Contract Development:

- **Drafting:** Draft the contract document incorporating agreed-upon terms, conditions, scope of work, deliverables, milestones, acceptance criteria, and legal provisions.
- **Legal Review:** Review the draft contract with legal counsel to ensure compliance with regulatory requirements, mitigate legal risks, and protect the interests of both parties.
- **Approval:** Obtain internal approvals from relevant stakeholders, including legal, finance, and senior management, before finalizing the contract.

4. Contract Execution:

- **Signing:** Once approved, arrange for the signing of the contract by authorized representatives from both the client and vendor organizations.
- **Contract Launch:** Communicate contract details, scope, expectations, and timelines to project teams and stakeholders involved in contract execution.

5. Contract Administration:

- **Implementation Planning:** Develop a detailed implementation plan outlining roles, responsibilities, timelines, and milestones for contract execution.
- **Monitoring and Control:** Establish mechanisms for monitoring vendor performance, tracking project progress, and ensuring adherence to contract terms and SLAs.
- **Issue Management:** Implement procedures for addressing issues, changes, disputes, and escalations that may arise during contract execution.

6. Performance Evaluation:

- **Performance Metrics:** Define and measure performance metrics and key performance indicators (KPIs) to assess vendor performance and project outcomes.
- **Reviews and Audits:** Conduct regular reviews, audits, and assessments to evaluate contract compliance, quality of deliverables, and achievement of project objectives.

7. Contract Closure:

- **Completion Verification:** Verify that all contractual obligations, deliverables, and acceptance criteria have been satisfactorily met.
- **Final Payment:** Process final payments or adjustments based on contract terms, including any penalties, incentives, or withholdings.
- **Lessons Learned:** Conduct a post-contract review to capture lessons learned, document successes, challenges, and recommendations for future contract placements.

Considerations for Success:

- **Communication:** Maintain open and transparent communication with vendors and stakeholders throughout the contract placement process.
- **Documentation:** Ensure comprehensive documentation of all contract-related communications, decisions, and agreements.
- **Risk Management:** Identify and mitigate potential risks associated with contract placement, performance, and compliance.
- **Flexibility:** Remain adaptable to changes in project scope, requirements, and external factors that may impact contract execution.

By following these stages in contract placement in software project management, organizations can effectively manage vendor relationships, mitigate risks, ensure project success, and achieve desired outcomes within defined timelines and budget constraints.

4.12 Typical Terms Of A Contract

In software project management, contracts typically include various terms and clauses that define the rights, responsibilities, obligations, and expectations of both parties involved—the client and the vendor. These terms are crucial for ensuring clarity, managing risks, and establishing a framework for project execution and delivery. Here are some typical terms found in contracts for software projects:

1. Scope of Work:

- **Description:** Defines the specific tasks, activities, and deliverables that the vendor is obligated to provide.
- **Details:** Includes detailed descriptions of software development activities, customization requirements, integration tasks, and any other services to be performed.

2. Project Timeline and Milestones:

- **Schedule:** Specifies the project timeline, key milestones, and deadlines for deliverables.
- **Dependencies:** Identifies dependencies and critical paths that impact project scheduling and completion.

3. Payment Terms:

- **Payment Schedule:** Outlines the schedule for payments to the vendor, typically based on milestones or project phases.
- **Rates and Fees:** Specifies the rates, pricing structure, and any additional fees or expenses reimbursable to the vendor.

4. Intellectual Property (IP) Rights:

- **Ownership:** Defines the ownership rights of intellectual property developed during the project, including software code, designs, documentation, and other deliverables.
- **License:** Specifies the terms under which the client can use the software and any limitations on distribution, modification, or resale.

5. Quality Assurance and Acceptance Criteria:

- **Quality Standards:** Sets forth the quality standards and criteria that the software must meet.
- **Acceptance Testing:** Describes the procedures and criteria for acceptance testing, including testing phases, environments, and acceptance criteria.

6. Change Management:

- **Change Control:** Establishes procedures for managing changes to project scope, requirements, and deliverables.
- **Change Requests:** Defines how change requests are submitted, evaluated, approved, and implemented.

7. Confidentiality and Data Security:

- **Confidentiality Obligations:** Specifies obligations to protect confidential information, trade secrets, and proprietary data.
- **Data Security:** Outlines measures for ensuring data security, including access controls, encryption, and compliance with data protection laws.

8. Termination and Suspension:

- **Termination Clause:** Specifies conditions under which either party may terminate the contract, such as breach of terms, failure to perform, or insolvency.
- **Suspension of Work:** Describes procedures for suspending project activities temporarily due to unforeseen circumstances or mutual agreement.

9. Warranties and Liabilities:

- **Performance Warranties:** Guarantees regarding the functionality, performance, and reliability of the software.
- **Limitation of Liability:** Limits the liability of each party for damages, losses, or liabilities arising from contract performance or non-performance.

10. Dispute Resolution:

- **Governing Law:** Specifies the jurisdiction and governing law that will apply to the contract.
- **Dispute Resolution:** Defines procedures for resolving disputes, including negotiation, mediation, arbitration, or litigation.

11. Insurance Requirements:

- **Insurance Coverage:** Specifies insurance requirements, such as professional liability insurance, to protect against potential risks and liabilities.

12. Subcontracting and Assignment:

- **Subcontracting:** Specifies whether the vendor can subcontract any part of the project and under what conditions.
- **Assignment:** Addresses whether the parties can assign their rights and obligations under the contract to another party.

13. Compliance with Laws and Regulations:

- **Regulatory Compliance:** Ensures compliance with applicable laws, regulations, and industry standards relevant to the project and software development.

14. Documentation and Deliverables:

- **Delivery Requirements:** Specifies the format, timing, and documentation requirements for deliverables, such as user manuals, training materials, and technical documentation.

15. Force Majeure:

- **Force Majeure Clause:** Defines unforeseen events or circumstances beyond the control of either party that may excuse non-performance temporarily.

These terms form the foundation of a software project contract, ensuring that both parties have a clear understanding of their responsibilities, obligations, and rights throughout the project lifecycle. Careful consideration and negotiation of these terms are essential to managing risks, protecting interests, and achieving successful outcomes in software project management.

4.13 Contract Management and Acceptance

In software project management, contract management and acceptance are critical processes that ensure both parties—the client and the vendor—adhere to agreed-upon terms and conditions and that deliverables meet specified requirements. Here's a detailed look at contract management and acceptance in software project management:

Contract Management:

Contract management involves overseeing the execution, administration, and monitoring of the contract throughout its lifecycle. This process ensures that the project progresses according to plan, risks are managed effectively, and both parties fulfill their contractual obligations. Key aspects of contract management include:

1. **Implementation Planning:**
   - Develop a detailed implementation plan that outlines roles, responsibilities, timelines, and milestones for contract execution.
   - Allocate resources and establish communication channels to support effective contract administration.
2. **Monitoring and Control:**
   - Monitor vendor performance, project progress, and adherence to contract terms, milestones, and quality standards.
   - Implement mechanisms for tracking deliverables, milestones, and expenditures against agreed-upon schedules and budgets.
3. **Issue Management:**
   - Establish procedures for addressing issues, changes, disputes, and escalations that may arise during contract execution.
   - Resolve conflicts promptly through effective communication, negotiation, and problem-solving.
4. **Documentation and Reporting:**
   - Maintain accurate and comprehensive documentation of all contract-related communications, decisions, and agreements.
   - Prepare regular progress reports, status updates, and performance evaluations for stakeholders and management review.
5. **Change Management:**
   - Manage changes to project scope, requirements, and deliverables through formal change control procedures.
   - Evaluate change requests, assess their impact on project objectives, and obtain necessary approvals before implementation.
6. **Contract Amendments and Renewals:**
   - Monitor contract expiration dates and renewal terms.
   - Negotiate and execute contract amendments as necessary to accommodate changes in project scope, schedule, or requirements.

Acceptance Management:

Acceptance management focuses on verifying that deliverables and milestones meet predefined acceptance criteria and quality standards before final acceptance by the client. It involves the following steps:

1. **Defining Acceptance Criteria:**
    - Establish clear and measurable criteria for evaluating deliverables, such as functionality, performance, usability, and compliance with specifications.
2. **Testing and Evaluation:**
    - Conduct acceptance testing to validate that deliverables meet the defined criteria and perform as expected in real-world scenarios.
    - Document test results, defects, and issues identified during testing.
3. **Client Review and Approval:**
    - Present deliverables to the client for review and approval based on acceptance criteria and test results.
    - Address client feedback, resolve any outstanding issues, and ensure alignment with client expectations.
4. **Formal Acceptance:**
    - Obtain formal acceptance or sign-off from the client once all acceptance criteria have been met and any required changes or corrections have been implemented.
    - Document acceptance through signed acceptance certificates or formal acceptance documents.
5. **Closure and Handover:**
    - Complete administrative tasks related to contract closure, such as finalizing payments, resolving outstanding issues, and transitioning deliverables to operational teams.
    - Conduct post-implementation reviews and lessons learned sessions to capture insights for future projects.

Importance of Contract Management and Acceptance:

- **Risk Mitigation:** Ensures that project risks are identified, assessed, and managed throughout the contract lifecycle.
- **Quality Assurance:** Verifies that deliverables meet quality standards and client expectations before final acceptance.
- **Stakeholder Alignment:** Facilitates effective communication and collaboration between stakeholders to achieve project goals.
- **Compliance and Accountability:** Ensures compliance with contractual obligations, regulatory requirements, and organizational policies.

- **Continuous Improvement:** Provides opportunities to learn from project experiences and improve contract management practices for future projects.

By effectively managing contracts and ensuring thorough acceptance processes in software project management, organizations can enhance project success, mitigate risks, and deliver valuable outcomes that meet client expectations and business objectives.

Chapter 5

MANAGING PEOPLE AND ORGANIZING TEAMS

Managing people and organizing teams in software project management is crucial for the success of projects in the dynamic and complex environment of software development. This aspect of project management focuses not only on technical aspects but also on harnessing human potential, fostering collaboration, and ensuring alignment with project goals. Here's an introduction to managing people and organizing teams in software project management:

Importance of Managing People and Organizing Teams

Software projects are inherently collaborative efforts that require diverse skill sets, expertise, and contributions from team members. Effective management of people and teams is essential for several reasons:

1. **Team Dynamics:** Software development often involves cross-functional teams comprising developers, designers, testers, and stakeholders. Managing these dynamics ensures efficient communication, coordination, and synergy among team members.
2. **Skill Utilization:** Each team member brings unique skills and experiences to the project. Effective management involves identifying and leveraging these skills to maximize productivity and creativity.
3. **Motivation and Engagement:** Motivated and engaged teams are more productive and innovative. Effective management fosters a positive work environment, supports professional growth, and aligns individual goals with project objectives.
4. **Risk Management:** People-related risks, such as turnover, conflicts, and communication breakdowns, can impact project timelines and outcomes. Effective management anticipates and mitigates these risks through proactive leadership and communication.
5. **Adaptability:** In software development, requirements and technologies evolve rapidly. Effective teams are adaptable, responsive to change, and capable of adjusting priorities and strategies as needed.

Strategies for Managing People and Organizing Teams

To effectively manage people and organize teams in software project management, consider the following strategies:

1. **Clear Roles and Responsibilities:**
   - Define clear roles, responsibilities, and expectations for each team member.
   - Ensure alignment between individual skills and project requirements.
2. **Effective Communication:**

   - Establish open and transparent communication channels within the team and with stakeholders.
   - Encourage feedback, active listening, and regular updates on project progress.
3. **Empowerment and Decision-Making:**
   - Empower team members to make decisions within their areas of expertise.
   - Foster a culture of trust, collaboration, and shared responsibility.
4. **Goal Alignment:**
   - Align individual goals with project objectives and organizational strategy.
   - Ensure team members understand how their contributions contribute to overall project success.
5. **Team Development:**
   - Invest in continuous learning and development opportunities for team members.
   - Support skills enhancement, certifications, and knowledge sharing within the team.
6. **Conflict Resolution:**
   - Address conflicts and disagreements promptly and constructively.
   - Use conflict resolution techniques to find mutually acceptable solutions.
7. **Performance Management:**
   - Monitor and evaluate team performance against project milestones and KPIs.
   - Provide regular feedback, recognize achievements, and address performance issues proactively.

Effective management of people and organizing teams is essential for achieving successful outcomes in software project management. By leveraging the strengths of team members, fostering collaboration, and maintaining clear communication, project managers can navigate challenges, drive innovation, and deliver high-quality software solutions that meet client expectations and business objectives. As software development methodologies evolve and projects become increasingly complex, the role of effective team management becomes even more critical in ensuring project success.

5.1 Understanding Behavior

Understanding behavior in managing people and organizing teams in software project management involves recognizing and addressing the human aspects that influence team dynamics, productivity, and project outcomes. Here's a deeper look into understanding behavior in this context:

Importance of Understanding Behavior

1. **Team Dynamics:** Behavior affects how team members interact, communicate, and collaborate. Understanding individual behaviors helps in fostering a positive team culture and improving overall team dynamics.
2. **Motivation and Engagement:** Different individuals are motivated by different factors. Understanding behaviors allows project managers to tailor motivational strategies that resonate with team members, enhancing engagement and commitment to project goals.
3. **Conflict Management:** Conflicts are inevitable in team settings. Understanding behavior helps in anticipating potential conflicts, addressing underlying issues, and promoting constructive conflict resolution strategies.
4. **Leadership Effectiveness:** Effective leadership requires an understanding of how behaviors influence team performance. Leaders who understand behavior can adapt their leadership styles to inspire and guide team members effectively.
5. **Decision Making:** Behavior influences how individuals perceive information, make decisions, and contribute to problem-solving. Understanding behavior facilitates more informed and inclusive decision-making processes within the team.

Key Aspects of Behavior in Software Project Management

1. **Personality Traits:**
   - Recognizing personality traits (e.g., introversion/extroversion, openness, conscientiousness) helps in assigning roles that align with individual strengths and preferences.
   - Understanding personality differences aids in managing communication styles and resolving conflicts.
2. **Communication Styles:**
   - Different team members may have varying communication preferences and styles.
   - Understanding these differences enables project managers to adapt communication strategies to ensure clarity, effectiveness, and inclusivity within the team.
3. **Motivation Factors:**
   - Identifying what motivates each team member (e.g., challenging tasks, recognition, career advancement) enhances motivation and improves individual and team performance.
   - Tailoring rewards and recognition programs based on individual preferences can boost morale and foster a positive work environment.
4. **Team Roles and Dynamics:**
   - Understanding behavioral tendencies helps in forming cohesive teams with complementary skills and abilities.

    - Assigning roles that leverage individual strengths and promote collaboration contributes to team effectiveness and project success.
5. **Conflict Resolution:**
    - Behavior influences how individuals respond to conflict and engage in resolution efforts.
    - Recognizing behavioral triggers and underlying causes of conflict enables project managers to facilitate constructive dialogue and find mutually acceptable solutions.

Strategies for Managing Behavior

1. **Building Relationships:** Foster trust and rapport among team members through team-building activities, open communication, and active listening.
2. **Clear Expectations:** Communicate clear goals, roles, and expectations to minimize misunderstandings and promote accountability.
3. **Feedback Mechanisms:** Establish regular feedback loops to provide constructive feedback, address concerns, and recognize achievements.
4. **Training and Development:** Provide opportunities for continuous learning and skills development to enhance individual capabilities and team performance.
5. **Conflict Resolution Skills:** Equip project managers and team members with conflict resolution skills and techniques to manage conflicts effectively and promote collaboration.

Understanding behavior in managing people and organizing teams is essential for creating a collaborative and productive environment in software project management. By recognizing individual differences, motivations, and communication styles, project managers can leverage team strengths, mitigate challenges, and achieve project objectives effectively. Ultimately, a deep understanding of behavior enables project managers to lead teams with empathy, adaptability, and responsiveness, contributing to the overall success of software projects.

5.2 Organizational Behaviour

Organizational Behavior (OB) provides a foundational framework for understanding how individuals, teams, and organizations function and interact within the context of software project management. In this domain, OB principles are instrumental in managing people, organizing teams, and optimizing organizational effectiveness. Here's an exploration of organizational behavior as it relates to managing people and organizing teams in software management:

Understanding Organizational Behavior

Organizational Behavior encompasses various aspects that influence individual and group behavior within an organization. Key elements include:

1. **Individual Behavior:**
   - **Personality and Attitudes:** Understanding individual differences in personality traits, values, attitudes, and perceptions helps project managers anticipate how team members might respond to challenges and opportunities.
   - **Motivation:** OB theories such as Maslow's Hierarchy of Needs and Herzberg's Two-Factor Theory guide managers in understanding what motivates individuals, whether it's intrinsic factors like recognition and achievement or extrinsic factors like compensation and job security.
   - **Decision-Making:** Behavioral economics and decision-making theories assist in understanding how individuals make choices, weighing risks, rewards, and uncertainties in software development projects.
2. **Group Dynamics:**
   - **Team Formation:** OB theories on team formation, such as Tuckman's stages of group development (forming, storming, norming, performing, adjourning), help project managers understand and navigate the stages teams go through.
   - **Communication:** Effective communication theories, including channels of communication and barriers to effective communication, are crucial for ensuring clear and efficient information flow within software project teams.
   - **Leadership:** Leadership theories (e.g., transformational, transactional, situational leadership) guide project managers in adopting appropriate leadership styles to motivate and lead software development teams effectively.
3. **Organizational Culture and Structure:**
   - **Culture:** Understanding organizational culture, including its values, norms, and beliefs, helps project managers align team behaviors and actions with organizational goals and objectives.
   - **Structure:** Organizational structure theories, such as mechanistic vs. organic structures, matrix organizations, and agile methodologies, inform project managers on how to design and adapt organizational structures that facilitate effective software project management.

Application in Managing People and Organizing Teams

In software project management, leveraging OB principles can enhance the management of people and the organization of teams in the following ways:

1. **Recruitment and Selection:**
    - Applying OB theories in job analysis and candidate assessment helps in selecting individuals who fit the organization's culture and possess the necessary skills and competencies for software development roles.
2. **Training and Development:**
    - Designing training programs based on OB principles ensures that team members acquire technical skills as well as interpersonal skills such as teamwork, communication, and conflict resolution, crucial for effective software project management.
3. **Team Building and Collaboration:**
    - Using OB theories on team dynamics and communication facilitates team building activities and fosters collaboration among diverse software development teams, improving productivity and innovation.
4. **Conflict Resolution and Negotiation:**
    - Applying OB theories on conflict resolution and negotiation helps project managers address conflicts constructively and facilitate win-win solutions in software development projects.
5. **Leadership and Motivation:**
    - Adopting effective leadership styles informed by OB theories motivates software development teams, enhances employee engagement, and drives project success.

Organizational Behavior provides a comprehensive understanding of human behavior within organizations, which is crucial for managing people and organizing teams in software project management. By applying OB principles, project managers can create a positive work environment, foster effective communication and collaboration, and align individual and team behaviors with organizational goals and project objectives. Ultimately, integrating OB concepts enhances team performance, drives innovation, and contributes to the overall success of software development projects

5.3 Selecting The Right Person For The Job

Selecting the right person for the job in software management is crucial for ensuring project success, team cohesion, and overall organizational effectiveness. Here's a detailed approach on how to select the right person for a software management role, focusing on managing people and organizing teams effectively:Steps to Selecting the Right Person for the Job

1. **Job Analysis and Role Definition:**

- **Define Job Requirements:** Conduct a thorough job analysis to identify the specific skills, competencies, qualifications, and experience required for the software management role. This includes technical skills (e.g., programming languages, software development methodologies), soft skills (e.g., communication, teamwork), and leadership qualities (e.g., decision-making, problem-solving).

- **Clarify Responsibilities:** Clearly define the roles, responsibilities, and expectations associated with the software management position. This ensures alignment between the job requirements and organizational goals.

2. **Recruitment Strategy:**

- **Targeted Search:** Develop a targeted recruitment strategy to attract candidates with the desired qualifications and expertise. This may include leveraging job boards, professional networks, industry associations, and referrals from existing employees.
- **Employer Branding:** Highlight the organization's culture, values, career opportunities, and unique selling points to attract top talent who align with the company's mission and vision.

3. **Selection Process:**

- **Resume Screening:** Review resumes and cover letters to shortlist candidates whose qualifications and experience match the job requirements.
- **Interviews:** Conduct structured interviews to assess candidates' technical skills, problem-solving abilities, communication skills, and cultural fit. Consider using behavioral interview questions to evaluate past performance and behavior in relevant situations.
- **Technical Assessments:** Administer technical assessments or coding challenges to evaluate candidates' proficiency in software development, problem-solving, and critical thinking skills.

4. **Assessment of Cultural Fit:**

- **Organizational Values:** Assess candidates for cultural fit with the organization's values, norms, and work environment. Consider how well candidates align with the company culture and their potential contributions to team dynamics and organizational culture.
- **Team Compatibility:** Evaluate candidates' interpersonal skills and ability to collaborate effectively with diverse teams. Assess their communication style, adaptability, and conflict resolution skills.

5. **Reference Checks and Background Verification:**

- **Reference Checks:** Contact references provided by candidates to verify their work experience, performance, and reliability. Seek insights into candidates' strengths, areas for development, and suitability for the software management role.

- **Background Verification:** Conduct background checks, including employment history, educational credentials, and professional certifications, to ensure candidates meet the organization's standards and legal requirements.

6. **Decision Making:**

- **Evaluation and Comparison:** Evaluate candidates based on their qualifications, performance in interviews and assessments, cultural fit, and references. Compare candidates against predefined selection criteria and prioritize those who best meet the job requirements and organizational needs.
- **Selection Committee:** Involve key stakeholders, such as senior management, department heads, and team members, in the decision-making process to gain diverse perspectives and consensus on the final selection.

7. **Offer and On boarding:**

- **Offer Negotiation:** Extend a competitive job offer to the selected candidate, including salary, benefits, and any additional incentives. Negotiate terms as needed to secure acceptance.
- **On boarding Process:** Develop an effective on boarding process to integrate the new hire into the software management role and organizational culture. Provide necessary training, orientation, and mentorship to facilitate a smooth transition and set expectations for performance and success.

Selecting the right person for the job in software management requires a strategic approach that considers both technical competencies and soft skills essential for effective leadership, teamwork, and project management. By conducting a thorough job analysis, implementing a targeted recruitment strategy, conducting comprehensive interviews and assessments, assessing cultural fit, and involving key stakeholders in the decision-making process, organizations can identify and onboard candidates who contribute positively to team dynamics, organizational goals, and overall project success in software management.

5.4 Instruction in the Best Methods

In software management, providing effective instruction in the best methods for managing people and organizing teams is crucial for achieving project success, fostering team collaboration, and maximizing organizational performance. Here are key aspects and strategies to consider when providing instruction in software management:

1. Training and Development Programs:

- **Technical Skills:** Offer training programs that enhance technical competencies relevant to software management roles, such as software development methodologies (e.g., Agile, Scrum), programming languages, version control systems, and software testing frameworks.
- **Soft Skills:** Include training on interpersonal skills essential for effective team management, such as communication, conflict resolution, negotiation, leadership, and decision-making skills.
- **Project Management:** Provide instruction in project management methodologies (e.g., Waterfall, Kanban, Lean) and tools (e.g., JIRA, Trello) to optimize project planning, execution, monitoring, and control processes.

2. Effective Communication and Collaboration:

- **Clear Communication:** Emphasize the importance of clear and concise communication among team members, stakeholders, and clients. Provide guidance on using appropriate communication channels and techniques (e.g., meetings, emails, instant messaging) to facilitate effective information sharing and decision-making.
- **Collaboration Tools:** Instruct teams on utilizing collaboration tools and platforms (e.g., Slack, Microsoft Teams, Zoom) to enhance virtual collaboration, document sharing, real-time communication, and project transparency.

3. Team Building and Leadership Development:

- **Team Dynamics:** Provide instruction on building cohesive and high-performing teams, including strategies for fostering trust, mutual respect, and accountability among team members. Encourage team bonding activities and cross-functional collaboration to strengthen relationships and improve teamwork.
- **Leadership Skills:** Offer leadership development programs that focus on coaching, mentoring, motivating, and empowering team members. Provide guidance on adaptive leadership styles that promote innovation, creativity, and resilience in software management.

4. Continuous Improvement and Adaptability:

- **Agile Practices:** Instruct teams on Agile principles and practices, such as iterative development, continuous integration, and sprint planning. Encourage teams to embrace Agile mindset and values to adapt quickly to changing project requirements and customer feedback.

- **Learning Culture:** Foster a culture of continuous learning and improvement by promoting knowledge sharing, attending conferences, workshops, and encouraging certifications relevant to software management and emerging technologies.

5. Performance Management and Feedback:

- **Goal Setting:** Provide guidance on setting SMART (Specific, Measurable, Achievable, Relevant, Time-bound) goals aligned with project objectives and organizational priorities.
- **Feedback Mechanisms:** Instruct managers on providing constructive feedback to team members regularly. Encourage two-way feedback to facilitate professional growth, identify areas for improvement, and recognize achievements.

6. Change Management and Adaptation:

- **Change Readiness:** Prepare teams for organizational changes, technology advancements, and market trends impacting software management. Instruct teams on change management strategies to minimize resistance, foster resilience, and ensure successful adaptation.

7. Ethical and Legal Considerations:

- **Compliance:** Provide instruction on ethical standards, data privacy laws, intellectual property rights, and cyber security best practices relevant to software management. Ensure teams understand and adhere to legal and regulatory requirements in software development and project delivery.

Effective instruction in the best methods for managing people and organizing teams in software management involves equipping teams with the necessary technical skills, fostering effective communication and collaboration, developing leadership capabilities, promoting continuous improvement, and preparing teams to navigate change and comply with ethical and legal standards. By investing in training, development programs, and promoting a supportive learning environment, organizations can empower teams to achieve project success, innovate, and deliver high-quality software solutions that meet customer expectations and business objectives.

5.5 Motivation

Motivation plays a pivotal role in software management as it directly impacts team performance, productivity, and overall project success. Effectively managing motivation involves understanding individual and team dynamics, identifying motivational factors, and implementing strategies to enhance engagement and satisfaction. Here's how motivation is crucial in managing people and organizing teams in software management:

Importance of Motivation in Software Management

1. **Enhanced Performance and Productivity:**
    - Motivated teams demonstrate higher levels of commitment and effort, leading to improved performance and increased productivity in software development projects.
    - Motivation encourages team members to strive for excellence, meet deadlines, and achieve project milestones efficiently.
2. **Retention and Talent Development:**
    - Motivated employees are more likely to stay with the organization, reducing turnover rates and retaining valuable talent within the software development team.
    - Continuous motivation contributes to talent development by fostering a learning culture and encouraging professional growth and skills enhancement.
3. **Innovation and Problem-Solving:**
    - Motivated teams are more creative and innovative, contributing to the development of novel solutions and improvements in software design, development processes, and problem-solving.
    - Motivation fosters a proactive mindset where team members actively seek opportunities to innovate and contribute to the success of software projects.

Strategies for Motivating Teams in Software Management

1. **Recognition and Rewards:**
    - Acknowledge and appreciate team members' contributions and achievements through verbal praise, awards, bonuses, or incentives tied to project milestones or individual performance.
    - Recognize both individual efforts and team accomplishments to foster a sense of pride and motivation among team members.
2. **Clear Goals and Expectations:**
    - Set clear, specific, and challenging goals that align with project objectives and organizational priorities. Ensure that goals are achievable and provide a sense of purpose and direction to team members.
    - Communicate expectations effectively and clarify roles and responsibilities within the team to reduce ambiguity and enhance motivation.
3. **Professional Development:**
    - Provide opportunities for skills development, training programs, certifications, and workshops that enhance technical expertise and professional growth in software development.
    - Support career advancement by offering mentorship, coaching, and opportunities to work on challenging projects that align with individual career aspirations.

4. **Empowerment and Autonomy:**
    - Delegate responsibilities and empower team members to make decisions, solve problems, and take ownership of their work.
    - Foster a supportive environment where team members feel empowered to voice their ideas, suggest improvements, and contribute to decision-making processes in software management.
5. **Team Collaboration and Communication:**
    - Promote open communication, transparency, and collaboration among team members to build trust, strengthen relationships, and enhance motivation.
    - Encourage teamwork through team-building activities, cross-functional collaboration, and knowledge sharing sessions that foster camaraderie and a sense of belonging.
6. **Feedback and Performance Reviews:**
    - Provide constructive feedback regularly to guide performance improvement, recognize achievements, and address areas for development.
    - Conduct performance reviews that focus on strengths, growth opportunities, and alignment with organizational values and goals to support continuous improvement and motivation.

Motivation is a dynamic force in software management that drives team performance, innovation, and organizational success. By understanding the diverse motivational factors that influence team members, and implementing effective strategies such as recognition, goal setting, professional development, empowerment, and feedback, software managers can create a motivating work environment where teams thrive, collaborate effectively, and deliver exceptional results in software development projects. Investing in motivation not only enhances individual and team performance but also contributes to long-term organizational success and competitiveness in the software industry.

5.6 The Old man

Managing older employees or team members in software management, here are some considerations:

Managing Older Employees in Software Management

1. **Recognize Experience and Expertise:**
    - Older employees often bring extensive industry knowledge, experience, and expertise to software projects. Acknowledge and leverage their insights to enhance team performance and project outcomes.

2. **Promote Continuous Learning:**
    - Encourage ongoing professional development opportunities for older employees to stay updated with emerging technologies, tools, and methodologies in software development.
    - Offer training programs, certifications, and workshops that support skill enhancement and career growth.
3. **Respect and Inclusivity:**
    - Foster a culture of respect and inclusivity where age diversity is valued and celebrated. Avoid age-related stereotypes or biases in decision-making and interactions within the team.
4. **Flexible Work Arrangements:**
    - Recognize that older employees may have different preferences or needs regarding work schedules or flexibility. Offer flexible work arrangements when feasible to accommodate their preferences.
5. **Mentorship and Leadership Opportunities:**
    - Provide mentorship opportunities for older employees to share their knowledge and mentor younger team members. Recognize their potential for leadership roles and encourage their involvement in leadership initiatives.
6. **Health and Well-being Support:**
    - Consider health and well-being initiatives that support older employees' physical and mental well-being. Offer resources or programs that promote work-life balance and overall wellness.
7. **Communication and Collaboration:**
    - Encourage open communication and collaboration across generations within the team. Facilitate knowledge sharing and constructive interactions that benefit from diverse perspectives and experiences.

Managing older employees in software management involves recognizing their valuable contributions, promoting continuous learning, fostering a supportive and inclusive work environment, and leveraging their experience to enhance team performance and achieve project success. By embracing age diversity and implementing strategies that cater to the needs and strengths of older employees, software managers can create a cohesive and productive team environment that thrives on collaboration, innovation, and mutual respect.

5.7 Hackman Job Characteristics Model

The Hackman and Oldham Job Characteristics Model is a framework developed to understand how job design influences employee motivation, satisfaction, and performance. It identifies key job characteristics that, when present, can lead to positive outcomes for employees in terms of their motivation and job satisfaction. Let's explore how this model can be applied in software management for managing people and organizing teams:

Hack man and Oldham Job Characteristics Model

The Job Characteristics Model identifies five core job characteristics that can make a job more motivating and satisfying:

1. **Skill Variety:**
   - In software management, offering tasks that require a variety of skills can enhance job satisfaction. For instance, software developers may be involved in coding, testing, debugging, and collaborating with others, ensuring they utilize multiple skills.
2. **Task Identity:**
   - Providing software developers with tasks that have identifiable outcomes can increase their sense of responsibility and ownership. For example, completing a module or feature within a software project allows them to see tangible results of their efforts.
3. **Task Significance:**
   - Emphasizing the importance of software development tasks within the larger project or organizational goals can motivate team members. Knowing that their work contributes meaningfully to the success of the project or organization enhances job satisfaction.
4. **Autonomy:**
   - Allowing software developers autonomy in how they approach and execute their tasks can boost motivation. Giving them the freedom to make decisions related to their work methods, problem-solving approaches, and task scheduling fosters a sense of empowerment.
5. **Feedback:**
   - Providing regular and constructive feedback on software developers' performance and progress is crucial. Feedback helps them understand how well they are performing, identify areas for improvement, and feel valued for their contributions.

Applying the Job Characteristics Model in Software Management

Job Design and Redesign:

- **Task Enrichment:** Use job design techniques such as task enrichment to incorporate more variety, autonomy, and feedback into software developers' roles. For example, involving them in decision-making processes related to project planning and execution.
- **Job Rotation:** Rotate software developers across different tasks or projects to broaden their skill set and increase task variety, while also allowing them to experience different levels of task significance.

Team Collaboration and Structure:

- **Team-based Tasks:** Design software projects that require collaboration among team members with complementary skills, enhancing task identity and significance.
- **Cross-functional Teams:** Form cross-functional teams where members from different departments or disciplines work together, fostering skill variety and task significance through diverse perspectives.

Leadership and Management Practices:

- **Empowerment:** Encourage participative decision-making and empower software developers to take ownership of their work, promoting autonomy and accountability.
- **Feedback Mechanisms:** Establish regular feedback loops through code reviews, sprint retrospectives, and performance evaluations to provide meaningful feedback that supports continuous improvement.

Benefits of Applying the Model

By applying the Job Characteristics Model in software management:

- **Increased Motivation:** Software developers are more likely to be motivated and engaged when their jobs offer meaningful tasks, autonomy, and opportunities for skill development.
- **Enhanced Job Satisfaction:** Providing clear task identities and significance, along with autonomy and feedback, contributes to higher job satisfaction among team members.
- **Improved Performance:** Motivated and satisfied software developers tend to perform better, leading to higher productivity, better quality of work, and successful project outcomes.

The Hackman and Oldham Job Characteristics Model provides a valuable framework for enhancing motivation, satisfaction, and performance among software developers and teams in software management. By designing jobs that incorporate skill variety, task identity, task significance, autonomy, and feedback, software managers can create a conducive work environment that promotes engagement, innovation, and overall success in software development projects.

5.8 Working in Groups

Working effectively in groups is essential in software management for managing people and organizing teams to achieve project success. Here are key considerations and strategies for fostering effective group dynamics in software management:

Importance of Working in Groups

1. **Collaborative Problem-Solving:**
    - Groups enable software teams to leverage diverse skills, knowledge, and perspectives to solve complex problems more effectively than individuals working alone.
    - Collaboration promotes creativity and innovation in software development by encouraging the exchange of ideas and solutions.
2. **Enhanced Communication:**
    - Working in groups facilitates open communication channels among team members, fostering transparency, clarity, and effective information sharing.
    - Communication within groups helps clarify project requirements, align goals, and coordinate tasks to ensure project deliverables meet stakeholders' expectations.
3. **Skill Utilization and Development:**
    - Groups allow individuals to contribute their specialized skills and expertise to different aspects of software development projects, maximizing skill utilization.
    - Working collaboratively in groups provides opportunities for skills development through knowledge sharing, peer learning, and constructive feedback.
4. **Shared Responsibility and Accountability:**
    - Group work promotes a sense of shared responsibility and accountability among team members for project outcomes and milestones.
    - Team members support each other, share workload responsibilities, and collectively strive towards achieving project goals.

Strategies for Effective Group Work in Software Management

1. **Establish Clear Goals and Roles:**
    - Define clear project goals, objectives, and roles within the group to ensure alignment with project requirements and organizational priorities.
    - Clarify individual responsibilities and expectations to minimize ambiguity and promote accountability among team members.
2. **Promote Team Building and Cohesion:**
    - Foster team building activities to build trust, rapport, and mutual respect among group members. This includes team-building exercises, social events, and collaborative problem-solving sessions.
    - Encourage open communication and create a supportive team environment where members feel comfortable sharing ideas and providing constructive feedback.
3. **Utilize Agile and Scrum Methodologies:**
    - Implement Agile methodologies such as Scrum or Kanban to organize group work into iterative cycles (sprints) with defined goals, tasks, and timelines.

   - Conduct regular stand-up meetings (daily scrums) to monitor progress, identify obstacles, and adapt plans accordingly to maintain momentum and productivity.
4. **Facilitate Effective Communication:**
   - Use communication tools and platforms (e.g., Slack, Microsoft Teams, Zoom) to facilitate real-time communication, file sharing, and collaboration among group members.
   - Establish communication norms and protocols to ensure information flows efficiently and effectively within the group and with stakeholders.
5. **Encourage Decision-Making and Problem-Solving:**
   - Foster a collaborative decision-making process where group members participate in discussing alternatives, evaluating options, and reaching consensus on project decisions.
   - Encourage critical thinking and problem-solving skills among team members to address challenges and optimize solutions in software development.
6. **Provide Constructive Feedback and Recognition:**
   - Foster a culture of continuous improvement by providing constructive feedback on individual and group performance.
   - Recognize and celebrate achievements, milestones, and contributions to reinforce positive behaviors and motivate team members.

Challenges and Mitigation Strategies

- **Conflict Resolution:** Anticipate and address conflicts that may arise within groups promptly through mediation, active listening, and negotiation to maintain team harmony and productivity.
- **Managing Diversity:** Embrace diversity within groups by valuing different perspectives, experiences, and cultural backgrounds to foster inclusivity and innovation.
- **Time Management:** Implement time management strategies, prioritize tasks, and allocate resources effectively to optimize group productivity and meet project deadlines.

Effective group work is fundamental in software management for managing people and organizing teams to achieve project success. By promoting collaborative problem-solving, enhancing communication, utilizing agile methodologies, facilitating decision-making, providing constructive feedback, and addressing challenges proactively, software managers can create a conducive environment where teams thrive, innovate, and deliver high-quality software solutions efficiently. Investing in effective group work practices fosters team cohesion, improves project outcomes, and enhances overall organizational performance in software development projects

5.9 Becoming a Team

Becoming a cohesive team in software management is a critical aspect of managing people and organizing teams effectively. Building a strong team involves fostering trust, collaboration, and shared goals among team members to achieve project success. Here's a comprehensive guide on how to become a team in software management:

1. Establish Clear Goals and Objectives:

- **Shared Vision:** Define a clear vision and mission for the team that aligns with organizational goals and project objectives in software management.
- **SMART Goals:** Set specific, measurable, achievable, relevant, and time-bound (SMART) goals to provide direction and focus for team efforts.

2. Build Trust and Rapport:

- **Open Communication:** Encourage open and transparent communication among team members. Create opportunities for team members to express their ideas, concerns, and feedback freely.
- **Team-building Activities:** Organize team-building exercises, workshops, or retreats to foster trust, build relationships, and strengthen camaraderie among team members.

3. Define Roles and Responsibilities:

- **Role Clarity:** Clarify individual roles, responsibilities, and expectations within the team. Ensure that each team member understands their contributions to the project and how they align with overall team objectives.
- **Cross-functional Collaboration:** Promote collaboration across different roles and disciplines within the software management team to leverage diverse skills and perspectives.

4. Promote Collaboration and Knowledge Sharing:

- **Collaborative Tools:** Utilize collaboration tools and platforms (e.g., project management software, communication apps) to facilitate real-time collaboration, document sharing, and task management.
- **Knowledge Sharing:** Encourage knowledge sharing sessions, peer mentoring, and cross-training opportunities to enhance collective expertise and skills development within the team.

5. Encourage Diversity and Inclusivity:

- **Value Diversity:** Embrace diversity in backgrounds, experiences, and perspectives within the team. Foster an inclusive environment where all team members feel respected, valued, and empowered to contribute.
- **Respectful Communication:** Promote respectful communication and active listening to ensure that every team member's voice is heard and considered in decision-making processes.

6. Support Continuous Learning and Growth:

- **Professional Development:** Provide opportunities for professional growth through training, certifications, workshops, and conferences relevant to software management and industry trends.
- **Feedback and Recognition:** Establish a culture of constructive feedback and recognition to acknowledge individual and team achievements, identify areas for improvement, and celebrate milestones.

7. Resolve Conflicts and Challenges:

- **Conflict Resolution:** Develop strategies and protocols for addressing conflicts constructively within the team. Encourage open dialogue, mediation, and compromise to resolve conflicts and maintain team cohesion.
- **Problem-Solving Skills:** Foster problem-solving skills among team members to collaboratively address challenges and overcome obstacles encountered in software management projects.

8. Empowerment and Decision-Making:

- **Empowerment:** Empower team members to take ownership of their work and make informed decisions within their areas of responsibility. Encourage autonomy and accountability to foster a sense of ownership and commitment.
- **Shared Decision-Making:** Involve team members in decision-making processes related to project planning, execution, and problem-solving. Seek consensus and leverage collective expertise to make informed decisions.

9. Celebrate Success and Learn from Failures:

- **Celebrate Achievements:** Recognize and celebrate team successes, achievements, and milestones to boost morale and reinforce positive behaviors.

- **Learning Culture:** Encourage a learning culture where team members reflect on both successes and failures, extract lessons learned, and apply insights to continuously improve processes and outcomes in software management.

Becoming a cohesive team in software management requires deliberate effort in building trust, fostering collaboration, defining roles, promoting inclusivity, supporting continuous learning, resolving conflicts, and empowering team members. By cultivating a shared vision, encouraging open communication, and nurturing a supportive team culture, software managers can create an environment where teams thrive, innovate, and deliver exceptional results in software development projects. Investing in team development enhances team effectiveness, boosts morale, and contributes to overall organizational success in software management

5.10 Decision Making

Decision making in software management, especially when managing people and organizing teams, is crucial for achieving project objectives, optimizing resources, and ensuring successful project outcomes. Effective decision-making processes involve a combination of analytical thinking, collaboration, consideration of stakeholder interests, and timely execution. Here's a comprehensive overview of decision-making in software management:

Importance of Decision Making in Software Management

1. **Project Success:**
    - Effective decision making ensures that the right choices are made throughout the software development lifecycle, from project initiation to delivery, to achieve project goals and meet client expectations.
    - Decisions impact project scope, timelines, resources, and quality, influencing overall project success and client satisfaction.
2. **Resource Optimization:**
    - Decisions regarding resource allocation, budget management, and task prioritization optimize resource utilization and maximize efficiency within software management.
    - Strategic resource allocation supports project scalability, minimizes costs, and enhances productivity.
3. **Risk Management:**
    - Decision making involves identifying, assessing, and mitigating risks associated with software projects. Proactive decision-making strategies minimize potential risks and uncertainties, ensuring project continuity and resilience.
    - Risk-aware decisions promote adaptive planning and facilitate timely responses to changing project requirements and external factors.

4. **Team Collaboration:**
    - Decision-making processes encourage collaborative engagement among software management teams, fostering collective problem-solving, knowledge sharing, and innovation.
    - Inclusive decision-making practices leverage diverse perspectives, promote team cohesion, and enhance decision quality through consensus-building and mutual understanding.

Effective Decision-Making Strategies in Software Management

1. **Data-Driven Analysis:**
    - Utilize data analytics, metrics, and performance indicators to inform decision-making processes in software management.
    - Analytical tools and techniques facilitate evidence-based decision making, enabling stakeholders to evaluate options, predict outcomes, and optimize decision outcomes.
2. **Collaborative Approach:**
    - Foster a collaborative decision-making environment where stakeholders, including project managers, developers, clients, and end-users, participate in discussions, share insights, and contribute to decision-making processes.
    - Encourage transparency, active listening, and constructive feedback to align stakeholders' interests and preferences with project objectives.
3. **Decision-Making Frameworks:**
    - Implement decision-making frameworks such as SWOT analysis (Strengths, Weaknesses, Opportunities, Threats), cost-benefit analysis, and risk assessment models to assess decision impacts and evaluate alternatives.
    - Structured frameworks guide systematic evaluation, prioritization, and implementation of decisions in software management.
4. **Agile Decision Making:**
    - Embrace Agile methodologies (e.g., Scrum, Kanban) that emphasize iterative development cycles, adaptive planning, and continuous improvement.
    - Agile frameworks support responsive decision making, enabling teams to adjust project priorities, address emerging issues, and deliver incremental value to stakeholders.
5. **Change Management:**
    - Implement change management strategies to anticipate, plan for, and effectively manage changes in software management projects.

- Decision-making processes should accommodate dynamic project environments, enabling teams to navigate change, mitigate disruptions, and maintain project alignment with organizational goals.

6. **Decision Review and Evaluation:**
    - Conduct post-decision reviews and evaluations to assess decision outcomes, identify lessons learned, and refine decision-making strategies in future software management projects.
    - Continuous improvement initiatives optimize decision-making processes, enhance organizational learning, and foster adaptive decision-making capabilities.

Effective decision making in software management is integral to project success, resource optimization, risk management, and team collaboration. By leveraging data-driven analysis, fostering collaboration, employing decision-making frameworks, embracing Agile methodologies, managing change effectively, and conducting post-decision evaluations, software managers can enhance decision quality, drive project efficiency, and achieve sustainable outcomes in software development projects. Investing in robust decision-making processes empowers teams to navigate complexities, capitalize on opportunities, and deliver value-driven solutions that meet client expectations and drive organizational growth in software management

5.11 Leadership

Leadership in software management involves guiding and inspiring teams to achieve project goals effectively while nurturing a positive and productive work environment. Effective software managers must demonstrate strong leadership qualities to motivate, empower, and support their teams through various stages of project development. Here's an exploration of leadership in software management, focusing on managing people and organizing teams:

Qualities of Effective Leadership in Software Management

1. **Visionary Thinking:**
    - **Strategic Direction:** Provide a clear vision and strategic direction for software projects, aligning team efforts with organizational goals and client expectations.
    - **Innovation:** Foster a culture of innovation and creativity by encouraging team members to explore new ideas, technologies, and solutions in software development.
2. **Communication Skills:**
    - **Clarity and Transparency:** Communicate goals, expectations, and project updates clearly to ensure alignment and understanding among team members.
    - **Active Listening:** Practice active listening to understand team concerns, gather feedback, and address issues promptly to maintain morale and motivation.

3. **Team Building and Motivation:**
    - **Empowerment:** Empower team members by delegating responsibilities, promoting autonomy, and providing opportunities for professional growth and development.
    - **Recognition:** Recognize and celebrate individual and team achievements to foster a positive work environment and boost team morale in software management.
4. **Decision Making and Problem Solving:**
    - **Strategic Decision Making:** Make informed decisions based on data, analysis, and stakeholder input to drive project success and mitigate risks in software management.
    - **Problem Solving:** Facilitate collaborative problem-solving sessions to address challenges, resolve issues, and optimize project outcomes effectively.
5. **Adaptability and Resilience:**
    - **Agility:** Embrace Agile methodologies and adaptive leadership practices to respond proactively to changes, uncertainties, and evolving project requirements in software management.
    - **Resilience:** Demonstrate resilience in navigating setbacks, managing conflicts, and maintaining team morale during challenging project phases.
6. **Ethical Leadership:**
    - **Integrity:** Uphold ethical standards, transparency, and accountability in decision making and interactions with team members, clients, and stakeholders.
    - **Fairness:** Promote fairness, equity, and inclusivity within the team, respecting diverse perspectives and fostering a culture of mutual respect in software management.

Strategies for Effective Leadership in Software Management

1. **Empowering Teams:**
    - Delegate tasks and responsibilities effectively, allowing team members to take ownership and contribute their expertise to software projects.
    - Encourage initiative and innovation by creating a supportive environment where team members feel empowered to propose and implement creative solutions.
2. **Building Relationships:**
    - Foster strong relationships based on trust, respect, and collaboration among team members, promoting a cohesive and high-performing team culture.
    - Develop rapport with stakeholders, clients, and external partners to facilitate effective communication and collaboration in software management.

3. **Continuous Learning and Development:**
    - Support continuous learning and skills development initiatives to enhance team capabilities, technical proficiency, and professional growth in software management.
    - Provide mentoring, coaching, and training opportunities that align with individual career goals and organizational objectives.
4. **Leading by Example:**
    - Demonstrate commitment, dedication, and perseverance in pursuing project goals and overcoming challenges, inspiring team members to strive for excellence.
    - Model ethical behavior, professionalism, and a strong work ethic to set a positive example and foster a culture of accountability and integrity in software management.
5. **Feedback and Performance Management:**
    - Implement regular feedback mechanisms and performance reviews to provide constructive feedback, recognize achievements, and address areas for improvement effectively.
    - Foster a culture of continuous improvement where feedback is valued, and lessons learned are applied to enhance project delivery and team performance in software management.

Effective leadership in software management is essential for guiding teams, driving project success, and fostering a collaborative and supportive work environment. By embodying visionary thinking, strong communication skills, team building, motivational leadership, strategic decision making, adaptability, ethical standards, and continuous learning, software managers can inspire teams to achieve their full potential and deliver high-quality software solutions. Investing in leadership development and practicing effective leadership strategies empower software managers to navigate complexities, inspire innovation, and achieve sustainable success in managing people and organizing teams in software management

5.12 Organizational Structures

Organizational structures in software management play a critical role in managing people and organizing teams effectively. The structure defines how roles, responsibilities, and communication channels are organized within an organization or a project team. Different organizational structures have unique advantages and considerations in software management. Here are some common organizational structures used in managing people and organizing teams in software management:

1. Functional Structure

- **Description:** In a functional structure, teams are organized based on specialized functions or departments, such as development, testing, design, and support.
- **Advantages:**
    - **Specialization:** Allows for deep expertise and specialization within functional areas.
    - **Efficiency:** Streamlines processes and improves efficiency within each functional unit.
    - **Clear Career Paths:** Provides clear career paths and development opportunities within specific functions.
- **Considerations:**
    - **Coordination:** Coordination across functions may be challenging, potentially leading to silos or communication barriers.
    - **Flexibility:** May lack flexibility in responding to rapidly changing project requirements or client needs.

2. Project-Based Structure

- **Description:** Teams are organized around specific projects or client engagements, with each project team having its own dedicated resources.
- **Advantages:**
    - **Focus:** Ensures alignment of resources, skills, and efforts towards achieving project objectives.
    - **Client-Centric:** Tailors teams and resources to meet specific client requirements and project deliverables.
    - **Adaptability:** Allows for flexibility and scalability based on project size and complexity.
- **Considerations:**
    - **Resource Allocation:** Resources may be spread thin across multiple projects, affecting availability and workload management.
    - **Team Stability:** Project teams disband after project completion, potentially impacting team continuity and knowledge retention.

3. Matrix Structure

- **Description:** Combines elements of both functional and project-based structures, where team members report to both functional managers (e.g., development manager) and project managers simultaneously.

- **Advantages:**
    - **Resource Optimization:** Allows for efficient resource utilization across multiple projects while maintaining functional expertise.
    - **Cross-Functional Collaboration:** Facilitates collaboration and knowledge sharing across different functional teams.
    - **Balance:** Balances project-specific goals with functional objectives and priorities.
- **Considerations:**
    - **Complexity:** Increases complexity in reporting relationships and decision-making processes.
    - **Conflict Resolution:** Potential for conflicts between project managers and functional managers over resource priorities and project deadlines.

4. Agile/Scrum Team Structure

- **Description:** Agile methodologies such as Scrum organize teams into cross-functional units (Scrum teams) with roles like Scrum Master, Product Owner, and Development Team.
- **Advantages:**
    - **Collaboration:** Promotes collaboration, transparency, and adaptive planning within self-managed teams.
    - **Iterative Development:** Supports iterative development cycles (sprints) focused on delivering incremental value and responding to feedback.
    - **Flexibility:** Emphasizes responsiveness to changing customer needs and evolving project requirements.
- **Considerations:**
    - **Team Dynamics:** Requires strong team cohesion, communication skills, and collaboration to function effectively.
    - **Skill Balance:** Ensuring a balance of skills within the Scrum team to address all aspects of software development.

Choosing the Right Structure in Software Management

- **Project Scope and Complexity:** Consider the scope, size, and complexity of software projects when selecting an organizational structure.
- **Client Requirements:** Align the structure with client requirements and project deliverables to ensure effective delivery and client satisfaction.
- **Team Dynamics:** Evaluate team dynamics, communication needs, and collaboration requirements to determine the most suitable structure.
- **Organizational Culture:** Consider the organization's culture, values, and leadership style in choosing an appropriate structure that aligns with overall strategic goals.

Choosing the right organizational structure in software management is crucial for managing people and organizing teams effectively. Each structure offers unique advantages and considerations, impacting project efficiency, team collaboration, and overall project success. By understanding the characteristics and implications of different organizational structures, software managers can make informed decisions to optimize team performance, enhance project outcomes, and align organizational goals with client expectations in software management

5.13 Stress

Stress management is crucial in software management when it comes to managing people and organizing teams effectively. Software development projects often involve tight deadlines, complex technical challenges, and high expectations from clients and stakeholders. Stress can impact team performance, productivity, and overall well-being. Here's how stress manifests in software management and strategies to manage it:

Sources of Stress in Software Management

1. **Workload and Deadlines:**
   - **Tight Schedules:** High-pressure environments with tight deadlines can lead to stress among team members, especially developers and project managers.
   - **Overcommitment:** Taking on too many projects or tasks simultaneously can overwhelm team members and contribute to stress.
2. **Technical Challenges:**
   - **Complexity:** Dealing with complex technical issues, bugs, or integration challenges can be stressful, particularly when solutions are not immediately apparent.
   - **Skill Gaps:** Lack of expertise or resources to address technical requirements can increase stress levels within the team.
3. **Uncertainty and Change:**
   - **Scope Changes:** Changes in project scope, requirements, or priorities can create uncertainty and stress, requiring teams to adapt quickly.
   - **Market Dynamics:** External factors such as competitive pressures or shifts in technology trends may introduce uncertainty and stress.
4. **Communication and Collaboration:**
   - **Team Dynamics:** Poor communication, conflicts, or misunderstandings among team members can escalate stress levels and impact team cohesion.
   - **Remote Work Challenges:** Virtual teams may face additional stressors related to communication barriers, time zone differences, and collaboration tools.
5. **Client Expectations:**
   - **Pressure to Deliver:** Meeting client expectations and delivering high-quality software solutions on time can create stress, especially in client-facing roles.

- **Feedback and Revisions:** Dealing with client feedback, revisions, and change requests can add pressure to project timelines and team dynamics.

Strategies for Managing Stress in Software Management

1. **Promote Work-Life Balance:**
    - **Flexible Schedules:** Offer flexible work arrangements and realistic project timelines to support work-life balance and prevent burnout.
    - **Encourage Breaks:** Encourage team members to take regular breaks, vacations, and time off to recharge and rejuvenate.
2. **Effective Workload Management:**
    - **Prioritization:** Use project management techniques (e.g., Agile methodologies) to prioritize tasks, manage workload, and allocate resources effectively.
    - **Capacity Planning:** Monitor team capacity and workload distribution to prevent overload and ensure equitable distribution of tasks.
3. **Clear Communication and Expectations:**
    - **Transparent Communication:** Foster open and transparent communication channels to clarify expectations, project goals, and roles within the team.
    - **Feedback Mechanisms:** Establish regular feedback loops and performance reviews to provide constructive feedback, recognize achievements, and address concerns proactively.
4. **Skill Development and Support:**
    - **Training and Development:** Invest in training programs and professional development opportunities to enhance technical skills, knowledge, and expertise within the team.
    - **Peer Support:** Foster a supportive team environment where team members can share experiences, seek advice, and collaborate on solutions to technical challenges.
5. **Stress Awareness and Resilience Building:**
    - **Stress Management Programs:** Implement stress management workshops, resilience training, or wellness initiatives to educate team members on stress management techniques and coping strategies.
    - **Mindfulness and Relaxation Techniques:** Encourage mindfulness practices, relaxation techniques, and stress-reducing activities (e.g., yoga, meditation) to promote well-being and resilience.
6. **Leadership and Support:**
    - **Empathetic Leadership:** Demonstrate empathy, support, and understanding towards team members' challenges and stressors.
    - **Conflict Resolution:** Address conflicts or issues within the team promptly and fairly to maintain a positive and collaborative work environment.

Stress management is essential in software management to ensure team well-being, productivity, and project success. By identifying sources of stress, implementing proactive strategies for stress reduction, promoting work-life balance, fostering effective communication, supporting skill development, and cultivating a supportive team culture, software managers can mitigate stressors effectively. Investing in stress management initiatives not only enhances team resilience and performance but also contributes to a positive work environment where team members can thrive and deliver exceptional results in software management.

5.14 Health and Safety

Health and safety considerations in software management are crucial for ensuring the well-being and productivity of team members. While software development is primarily an office-based activity, there are several health and safety factors that software managers should address to create a supportive and safe work environment. Here are key aspects to consider:

Physical Health Considerations

1. **Ergonomics:**
   - **Workspace Design:** Ensure workstations are ergonomically designed to support comfortable and healthy posture, including adjustable chairs, desks, and monitor heights.
   - **Equipment:** Provide ergonomic accessories such as wrist rests, footrests, and ergonomic keyboards to reduce strain and prevent repetitive stress injuries (RSIs).
2. **Eye Health:**
   - **Screen Time:** Encourage regular breaks and the use of the 20-20-20 rule (every 20 minutes, look at something 20 feet away for 20 seconds) to reduce eye strain from prolonged screen use.
   - **Lighting:** Optimize lighting conditions to reduce glare and ensure adequate lighting levels to prevent eye fatigue.
3. **Physical Activity:**
   - **Encouragement:** Promote physical activity breaks and movement throughout the workday to combat sedentary behavior and promote overall physical health.
   - **Wellness Programs:** Offer wellness initiatives, such as fitness challenges or onsite exercise classes, to encourage regular physical activity among team members.

Mental Health and Well-being

1. **Workload Management:**
   - **Balanced Workloads:** Ensure workload distribution is manageable and realistic, avoiding overburdening team members with excessive work demands.

- **Time Management:** Promote effective time management strategies to reduce stress and improve work-life balance.

2. **Stress Management:**
    - **Supportive Environment:** Foster a supportive work culture where team members feel comfortable discussing stressors and seeking support from colleagues and management.
    - **Stress Reduction Techniques:** Provide resources and encourage stress reduction techniques such as mindfulness, meditation, and relaxation exercises.
3. **Workplace Culture:**
    - **Open Communication:** Establish open communication channels for discussing mental health concerns, promoting psychological safety, and reducing stigma associated with mental health issues.
    - **Training and Awareness:** Conduct training sessions or workshops on mental health awareness, stress management, and resilience building for all team members.

Environmental Safety

1. **Workspace Environment:**
    - **Air Quality:** Ensure good indoor air quality with proper ventilation systems and regular maintenance to prevent health issues related to poor air circulation.
    - **Temperature Control:** Maintain comfortable temperature levels within the workspace to enhance comfort and productivity.
2. **Safety Protocols:**
    - **Emergency Procedures:** Educate team members on emergency procedures, including evacuation routes, first aid kits, and protocols for handling workplace accidents or incidents.
    - **Equipment Safety:** Regularly inspect and maintain office equipment, including computers, electrical outlets, and cables, to prevent potential hazards or accidents.

Remote Work Considerations

1. **Home Office Setup:**
    - **Guidelines:** Provide guidelines or resources for setting up a safe and ergonomic home office environment, including recommendations for furniture and equipment.
2. **Virtual Well-being Support:**
    - **Virtual Wellness Programs:** Offer virtual wellness programs, mental health resources, and remote team-building activities to support the well-being of remote team members.

Compliance and Support

1. **Legal Compliance:**
   - **Health and Safety Regulations:** Ensure compliance with local health and safety regulations, including ergonomic standards and workplace safety guidelines.
   - **Policies and Procedures:** Develop and communicate health and safety policies, procedures, and guidelines tailored to the specific needs and challenges of software management.
2. **Support Systems:**
   - **Employee Assistance Programs (EAPs):** Provide access to EAPs or counseling services for confidential support and guidance on health, wellness, and mental health concerns.
   - **Managerial Support:** Equip managers with training and resources to effectively support team members' health and safety needs, including recognizing signs of stress or burnout.

Health and safety in software management encompass a range of physical, mental, and environmental considerations aimed at promoting a safe, supportive, and productive work environment. By addressing ergonomic practices, mental health support, environmental safety, compliance with regulations, and promoting a culture of well-being, software managers can enhance team health, morale, and performance in managing people and organizing teams effectively. Prioritizing health and safety initiatives not only mitigates risks and enhances productivity but also fosters a positive workplace culture where team members feel valued, supported, and empowered to contribute to organizational success in software management

5.15 Case Studies

Case studies in software management provide valuable insights into real-world scenarios, challenges, and solutions encountered in managing people and organizing teams within the software development context. These studies illustrate various aspects of leadership, team dynamics, project management, and organizational strategies. Here are a few examples of potential case studies in software management:

1. Project Management and Team Dynamics

Case Study: Managing a Complex Software Development Project

- **Scenario:** A software company embarks on a project to develop a new enterprise application for a client in a highly regulated industry.

- **Challenges:** Tight deadlines, changing requirements, and integration complexities pose significant challenges. Team members face communication barriers due to cultural differences between onshore and offshore teams.
- **Strategies:**
    - Implement Agile methodologies to promote flexibility and responsiveness to changing requirements.
    - Foster cross-cultural understanding through team-building activities and virtual collaboration tools.
    - Establish clear communication channels and regular progress meetings to enhance transparency and alignment.

2. Leadership and Decision Making

Case Study: Leadership Challenges in a Software Startup

- **Scenario:** A startup company faces rapid growth and scaling challenges while maintaining a startup culture and innovation.
- **Challenges:** Leadership must balance technical innovation with operational efficiency. Team members struggle with role clarity and adapting to evolving project priorities.
- **Strategies:**
    - Implement a flat organizational structure with empowered, self-managed teams to foster innovation and agility.
    - Invest in leadership development and mentorship programs to support emerging leaders and promote a culture of continuous learning.
    - Enhance decision-making processes through data-driven insights and stakeholder collaboration to align with strategic goals.

3. Agile Transformation

Case Study: Agile Transformation in a Large Enterprise

- **Scenario:** A large financial institution undertakes an agile transformation initiative to enhance software delivery speed and responsiveness.
- **Challenges:** Resistance to change from traditional waterfall methodologies, siloed organizational structure, and cultural barriers to Agile adoption.
- **Strategies:**
    - Conduct comprehensive Agile training programs and workshops for teams and leadership to build understanding and support for Agile principles and practices.
    - Establish Agile CoEs (Centers of Excellence) to provide coaching, guidance, and support for Agile teams across the organization.

    - Foster a culture of experimentation and continuous improvement by celebrating successes and learning from failures during the Agile transformation journey.

4. Remote Team Management

Case Study: Managing Distributed Software Teams

- **Scenario:** A software development company adopts a remote-first policy due to global workforce trends and technological advancements.
- **Challenges:** Remote team members face communication challenges, time zone differences, and maintaining team cohesion and motivation.
- **Strategies:**
    - Implement robust communication and collaboration tools to facilitate virtual meetings, instant messaging, and document sharing.
    - Establish clear expectations and guidelines for remote work policies, including work hours, availability, and deliverables.
    - Promote virtual team-building activities, such as virtual coffee breaks, online games, and informal social gatherings, to foster team bonding and morale.

5. Crisis Management

Case Study: Crisis Management in Software Development

- **Scenario:** A critical security vulnerability is discovered in a widely used software application developed by a technology company.
- **Challenges:** Urgent response required to patch the vulnerability, communicate with stakeholders, and restore trust in the product.
- **Strategies:**
    - Activate a cross-functional crisis management team with representatives from development, QA, security, legal, and communications departments.
    - Develop and execute a rapid response plan, including patch development, testing, and deployment, while maintaining service continuity.
    - Communicate transparently with customers, stakeholders, and the public through proactive communication channels and updates.

Case studies in software management provide valuable learning opportunities by examining real-world experiences, successes, and challenges faced by organizations in managing people and organizing teams in software development projects. These studies offer practical insights into effective leadership, team collaboration, project management methodologies, Agile transformations, crisis management, and remote team management strategies. By analyzing case studies, software managers can glean best practices, lessons learned, and innovative solutions to apply in their own organizational contexts, driving continuous improvement and enhancing project outcomes in software management.

References

1. "Software Project Survival Guide" by Steve McConnell - This book provides practical advice and techniques for managing software projects effectively, covering planning, scheduling, tracking progress, and managing risks.
2. "Agile Estimating and Planning" by Mike Cohn - Focuses on agile methodologies and provides guidance on how to estimate and plan agile projects effectively.
3. "The Mythical Man-Month: Essays on Software Engineering" by Frederick P. Brooks Jr. - A classic book that discusses the challenges of managing software projects, including scheduling, team dynamics, and productivity.
4. "Scrum: The Art of Doing Twice the Work in Half the Time" by Jeff Sutherland - Offers insights into Scrum methodology, which is widely used in software development for managing projects iteratively and incrementally.
5. "Managing the Unmanageable: Rules, Tools, and Insights for Managing Software People and Teams" by Mickey W. Mantle and Ron Lichty - Focuses on the human aspects of managing software projects, including team dynamics, leadership, and collaboration.
6. "The Art of Project Management" by Scott Berkun - Provides practical advice on managing projects, including software projects, covering topics such as planning, communication, and dealing with challenges.
7. "Effective Project Management: Traditional, Agile, Extreme" by Robert K. Wysocki - Offers a comprehensive overview of different project

management methodologies, including agile and traditional approaches, with practical guidance on implementation.

8. "Agile Project Management with Scrum" by Ken Schwaber - Another excellent resource on Scrum methodology, focusing on practical application and best practices.
9. "Lean Software Development: An Agile Toolkit" by Mary Poppendieck and Tom Poppendieck - Explores lean principles applied to software development, emphasizing efficiency, eliminating waste, and continuous improvement.
10. "Project Management for Software Development" by James A. Crowder and Shelli Friess - Covers project management principles specifically tailored to software development projects, with practical examples and case studies.

www.ingramcontent.com/pod-product-compliance
Ingram Content Group UK Ltd.
Pitfield, Milton Keynes, MK11 3LW, UK
UKHW060125010826
14089UKWH00006B/160

9 798895 197387